MUSIC & DRAMA LIBRARY
TROW. 2713

Themes from Life

Graham Stoate

Head of Drama
Purbeck School, Wareham, Dorset

Nelson Harrap

Thomas Nelson and Sons Ltd
Nelson House Mayfield Road
Walton-on-Thames Surrey
KT12 5PL UK

51 York Place
Edinburgh
EH1 3JD UK

Thomas Nelson (Hong Kong) Ltd
Toppan Building 10/F
22A Westlands Road
Quarry Bay Hong Kong

Thomas Nelson (Kenya) Ltd
P.O. Box 18123
Nairobi Kenya

Distributed in Australia by
Thomas Nelson Australia
480 La Trobe Street
Melbourne Victoria 3000
and in Sydney, Brisbane, Adelaide and Perth

© Graham Stoate 1983

First published by Harrap Limited 1983
(under ISBN 0-245-53998-0)

Second impression published by Thomas Nelson and Sons Ltd 1985

ISBN 0-17-444167-3
NCN 02
Printed in Great Britain by Mackays of Chatham Ltd

All Rights Reserved. This publication is protected in the United Kingdom by the Copyright Act 1956 and in other countries by comparable legislation. No part of it may be reproduced or recorded by any means without the permision of the publisher. This prohibition extends (with certain very limited exceptions) to photocopying and similar processes, and written permission to make a copy or copies must therefore be obtained from the publisher in advance. It is advisable to consult the publisher if there is any doubt regarding the legality of any proposed copying.

Contents

Acknowledgements

The Author would like to acknowledge, with grateful thanks, the support and encouragement of his wife and family, and colleagues at Purbeck Upper School, particularly those in the Drama and English Departments.

We are grateful to the following for permission to reproduce extracts from their publications:
Amber Lane Productions Ltd and Brian Clark for his play *Whose Life is it Anyway?*, published by Amber Lane Press; Jonathan Cape Ltd for *The Kitchen* by Arnold Wesker; Sheila Lemon Ltd for *Kes* by Barry Hines and Allan Stronach, originally published by Michael Joseph Ltd; Methuen London and Harold Pinter for his play *Last to Go*; Methuen London and Stephen Poliakoff for his play *City Sugar*; William Morris Agency Ltd for *The Innocent Must Suffer* from *Talking to a Stranger* by John Hopkins, published by Penguin Books Ltd; A.D. Peters & Co Ltd for *Abigail's Party* by Mike Leigh; Margaret Ramsay Ltd for *Mother Figure* from *Confusions* by Alan Ayckbourn (All rights in this play are strictly reserved and application for performance, etc., should be made before rehearsal to Margaret Ramsay Ltd., 14A Goodwin's Court, St Martin's Lane, London WC2N 4LL. No performance may be given unless a licence has been obtained); Margaret Ramsay Ltd for *Zigger Zagger* by Peter Terson, published by Penguin Books Ltd; Barry Reckord for his play *Skyvers*, published by Penguin Books Ltd; N.F. Simpson for his play *One Blast and Have Done*, published by Faber and Faber; Harvey Unna & Stephen Durbridge Ltd for *A Many Splendoured Thing* and *Marital Union* from *England our England* by Keith Waterhouse and Willis Hall.

Photographs
Richard and Sally Greenhill page 7 top left, bottom left; Keystone press page 7 top right, page 57 top right, page 81 top left; Derek Bishton at Sidelines page 7 bottom right; Keith Hawkins page 41 (both); Tesco Supermarkets page 57 top left; Big Star Pictures page 57 bottom left; Grand Metropolitan Catering page 57 bottom right; Commissioner of Police of the Metropolis page 81 top right; Thames Television page 81 bottom left; Topham Picture Library page 81 bottom right; John Vere Brown page 119

Introduction

> . . . all this life of mortal man, what is it but a kind of stage play, where men come forth, disguised one in one array, and another in another, each playing his part?
>
> Erasmus, *In Praise of Folly*

For centuries writers, searching for an original way of describing human life, have compared it to a stage play. Shakespeare, to take another example, wrote:

> All the world's a stage,
> And all the men and women merely players,
> They have their exits and their entrances,
> And one man in his time plays many parts.
>
> *As You Like It*

It is hardly surprising, therefore, that when we see or read a play we usually find one aspect or another of 'this life of mortal man' portrayed within it.

Not all plays deal with 'themes from life'. They do not *all* debate social issues, examine human problems or explore human relationships. But the extracts from plays and the sketches in this book all share one common theme. They are all reflections of the life we lead now; of the real problems real people have to face in life, and the decisions, the frustrations, the joys and the sorrows we may encounter at some stage in our lives.

This book is designed primarily for use with Fourth and Fifth Year pupils of average ability upwards. It should also be appropriate for Sixth Form usage, particularly for those returning to take less academic courses. Its aim is to provide interesting, enjoyable and dramatically relevant material for reading or acting in the classroom or studio, with suitable questions for discussion and written work, together with suggestions for improvisations or script writing.

There is no substitute for reading a play in entirety, but textual study of this sort, providing as it does a tantalising invitation to read the rest of the play, has other advantages too. These extracts and sketches provide a rich and varied model for language acquisition, oral and written, and for the improvement, by example, of improvisational techniques. They also provide a unique opportunity for group co-operation and involvement when students work on them, particularly if discussion assignments are sometimes carried out in small groups, possibly reporting back to the whole class afterwards.

Themes From Life will probably appeal to English and Drama teachers most, where it could be used as a sampler of contemporary drama, or as an introduction to the textual component of a Drama or Theatre Arts course. But because of its thematic content, it could also be used effectively in Social Studies, Social Education or Religious Education lessons as well.

Graham Stoate

Love, Marriage and Family Life

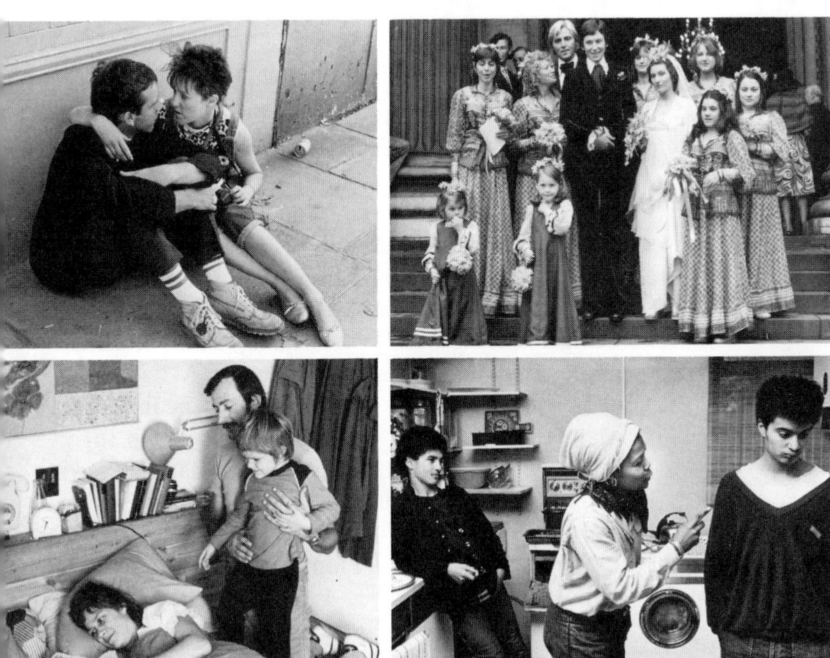

Many people think that finding a husband or wife and settling down in a family is one of the most important things in life. Do you agree? The plays in this section look at the themes of love, marriage and family life.

Use these pictures as starting points for improvisations, script work, or short stories. It is best to begin by deciding for yourself who these people are. Give them a complete identity: from naming them to giving them an exact age and personality. Then work out what is happening in the photograph you have chosen to work on, and go on from there.

Keith Waterhouse and Willis Hall

A Many Splendoured Thing

The playwrights Both Waterhouse and Hall were born in Leeds in 1929. Keith Waterhouse left school at fifteen and worked at various jobs before becoming a journalist. His career as a writer began with two novels: *There is a Happy Land* and *Jubb*. Willis Hall first wrote plays during his military service in Malaya for the Chinese Schools Department of Radio Malaya. On his return to England, he wrote many other plays, the most famous being *The Long and The Short and The Tall*, which made use of his wartime experience in Malaya. Waterhouse and Hall collaborated for the first time on a play called *Billy Liar* which was published in 1959. This began a productive partnership that resulted in many other successful plays and film scripts.

The play 'A Many Splendoured Thing' – a reference to a popular song about love – is one complete sketch from a revue called *England Our England*, which was first performed on 7 May 1962. A revue is a collection of songs, sketches, monologues or even dances and mimes, sometimes with a central theme. In this case, *England Our England* focused on aspects of contemporary British life. Even though it is now over twenty years since it was written, many of its themes are as relevant today as they were then.

The extract 'A Many Splendoured Thing' is set in the auditorium of a cinema, during the showing of a film. Two usherettes are standing at the back watching it and talking to each other at the same time. Behind their conversation, we hear background music from the film, interjected with dialogue from it.

Characters: how it might be acted

Joyce: *an usherette in her early twenties.*
Hettie: *the same, but a motherly woman in her forties.*
Hero/Heroine: *two voices on the film soundtrack.*

A simple set could be made with just one row of chairs to indicate the back row of the cinema, the two usherettes standing behind them looking out at the screen in front of them.

Try experimenting with accents to exploit the humour of this piece to the full. The Hero and Heroine, for example, could be Northern working class, and Joyce and Hettie Cockneys.

You might attempt to record the film soundtrack or it could be read live by two characters offstage. If you are staging this sketch, soft lighting on the faces of the two usherettes would give the effect of the light that would be reflected on them from the screen they are supposedly watching.

Two cinema usherettes, Joyce and Hettie, are standing at the back of a cinema, while the main feature film is showing. We hear a few lines from the screen hero and heroine before Joyce and Hettie speak.

. Many Splendoured Thing

Hero Haven't you ever sat on the canal with a bloke before?
(*Pause.*)

Heroine (*inexplicably breathless*) Like to know, wouldn't you?
(*Pause.*)

Hero You've got nice eyes. You've got a nice figure. (*With extreme diffidence as though nervous of the censor.*) Makes me—you know—want to touch you.
(*Long pause.*)

Heroine Nobody's stopping you.
(*There is a further pause before* **Joyce**, *who has been automatically chewing gum, speaks. Her voice is raucous and brassy. During their dialogue* **Joyce** *and* **Hettie** *never take their eyes from the screen.*)

Joyce I'm getting engaged on Monday.

Hettie Are you? What, to that ginger-headed feller?

Joyce Who? Jug-ears? (*With extreme scorn.*) No-o-o-o! No, it's another feller.

Hettie Lovely.

Joyce You know Hudson Verity's?

Hettie Yes?

Joyce Well, you know that mucky book shop next to it?
Hettie Yes?
Joyce Well, you know the pub next door?
Hettie Yes?
Joyce Well, you know them petrol pumps just opposite?
Hettie Yes?
Joyce Well, he works there.
Hettie Very nice.
(*They relapse into silence, and we hear a few more lines of dialogu from the screen.*)
Heroine (*more breathless than ever*) Don't, Harry—please don't.
Hero (*equally breathless*) I want you, Mary.
Heroine I want you as well—
(*A pause, during which we hear intriguing scuffling sounds.*)
Joyce Do you know how I met him? He cracked me on the back of th neck with a two-inch bolt. He did! No, 'cause I always walk pa there on my way to work. And I used to see this chap with crinkly hair. And every day when I walked past he used to flick nuts and bolts at me, so I knew he was interested. So I thought I won't speak, I'll let him speak first—you don't want to cheapen yourself. Then one day I'm walking past and there's this big iron bolt comes whizzing through the air and catches me right on the back of the neck! I went straight up to him and says: 'You bloody midden-tin,' I says, 'you do that again and you'll get my knee where you'll know about it for a long time to come!' He says, 'I wouldn't be much use to you then, would I?' I says, 'You're not much use now, you big gormless pig.' So, of course we started going out together.
Hettie (*without surprise*) Oh?
(*Pause.*)
Heroine (*in a voice of wonderment*) Harry, Harry—I feel different, Harry. I feel like a woman for the first time.
Hero (*brusquely*) Do you?
(*A futher pause and then* **Joyce** *flashes her torch on her neck.*)
Joyce (*conversationally*). See this mark on my neck? That's him biting Ooh, he's a mucky devil! We were just sitting in that bus shelte and he reckons he's having a sleep on my shoulder. (*Her voice rises disapprovingly.*) I says, 'Hey, hey, hey, what you doing?' He says, 'I'm giving you a love-bite.' I says, 'You filthy dog,' I says. 'I'll love-bite you.'
Hettie (*sententiously*) They're all the same, love. Out for what they can get.
Joyce Oh, he tries all sorts on. Got a one-track mind and that's dirt-track. (*Mimicking him in a jeering falsetto.*) 'Oooh, haven't you

got warm legs?' I says, 'Yes, and you've got cold hands, haven't you?' He says, 'Yes.' I says, 'Well, they won't be if I put this lighted cigarette on them.'
(*Another pause.*)

Heroine You won't leave me now, Harry, will you?
(*A silence. Her voice rises to a panic.*)
How we gunna manage? Where we gunna live?

Hero I don't know. What's it matter?

Joyce Supposed to be going for a walk last week—up to Middleton Woods. Hadn't been off the bus for five minutes and he's got his coat down. (*Mimicking again.*) 'Oooh, shall we sit down for five minutes?' (*With rising indignation.*) Broad daylight! Kissing and slobbering in the middle of the afternoon! I says, 'Don't you know there's a feller watching you?' He says, 'Where?' I says, 'Behind that tree. That gentleman with the glasses and the gaberdine raincoat.' I says, 'In any case, what have I got on my finger?' He says 'Nothing.' I says, 'Yes, and that's all you're getting till I get a ring on it.'

Hettie So when are you thinking of getting married, then?

Joyce Oh, sometime—no hurry.

Hettie You do right. You want to enjoy yourselves while you've got the chance. It'll be different when you're married. It's not all love and kisses then.
(*Pause.*)

Heroine I'll make you happy, Harry. If you'll only stay with me. You can do what you like with me. You can walk over me, if you want. I love you, Harry.
(*Pause.*)

Joyce (*cheerfully*) Oh, I know. It's not like the picture, is it?
Fade-out *as the film music comes to a crescendo.*

Points for discussion or written work

1. As the title seems to indicate, 'A Many Splendoured Thing' is about love. How does Joyce's experience of it differ from what is going on in the film? What is more true to life?

2. How does Hettie react to what she hears? Is her response genuine, do you think?

3. When Hettie says 'It'll be different when you're married. It's not all love and kisses then,' what do you think she means?

4. Would Joyce have had the same conversation with her mother? How might it have differed, and why?

5. Make a list of all the things you think are important in the ideal husband/wife. For example, looks, personality. Arrange the list in order of priority. Is money or job important? Do you have to share the same interests? Write a detailed description of your ideal partner.

6. What is it like when you meet someone for the first time? Do first impressions count? Do we judge people by their appearance and the way they dress?

7. Write a story about a pair of nervous teenagers on their first date. You could call it 'Blind Date'—or give it your own title.

8. Imagine you are Joyce writing to the Problem Page of a teenage magazine for advice about your boyfriend. Set out the letter properly, inventing a full name and address for Joyce, including as much information from the extract as possible. After you have done this, you could try writing a reply from the Editor of the Problem Page, or exchange your letter from Joyce with one written by someone else in your group, and write a reply to that.

Suggestions for script or improvisation

1. Improvise or script the scene where Hettie returns home from work and tells her husband Fred what Joyce had told her. Would she make her real views about Joyce known to him?

2. Improvise or script the scene between Joyce and her mother. While Joyce has been at the cinema that evening, Joyce's mother has been talking to a neighbour, Mrs Micklethwaite, who says she saw Joyce and her boyfriend in Middleton Woods. She decides to tackle Joyce about this as soon as she arrives home from work. You can decide the outcome!

Moving on from there . . .

3. Set up a scene for script or improvisation with a teenage daughter bringing a boyfriend home for the first time. There can be any number of characters, but as a minimum her family should include: Mum; Dad; and slightly younger brother or sister. Try to include differing attitudes to the boyfriend on the part of individual members of the family from one of warm welcome, to cool suspicion or even outright dislike.

4. Create a sketch showing the problems experienced by a young married couple who have been forced, for some reason, to live with one of their parents.

Alan Ayckbourn

Mother Figure

The playwright

Alan Ayckbourn was born in London in 1939 and, after leaving school at 17, made a start on a career in the theatre. He was in repertory at Worthing, Leatherhead Oxford and finally at Scarborough. From 1965 to 1969 he was a producer for BBC Radio Drama in Leeds, and since 1969 has been Director of Productions at the Library Theatre, Scarborough. His many successful plays include: *Relatively Speaking, Ernie's Incredible Illucinations, The Norman Conquests, Bedroom Farce*, and, most recently, *Season's Greetings.* Although written initially for the company at Scarborough, and performed there first, most of his plays transfer successfully to London's West End and to other regional theatres. Much of Ayckbourn's work is comedy; but the superior form of comedy which, while making its audience laugh, also makes it think.

The play

Mother Figure is the first of a set of five interlinked one-act plays, called *Confusions*, which deals humorously, but with sharply-pointed undertones, with human weaknesses and loneliness.

The extract

Mother Figure is set in an ordinary suburban sitting-room, described by Ayckbourn as being, 'fairly untidy, with evidence of small children'. The central character, Lucy, is a young mother who is often left alone for long periods with her children.

Characters: how it might be acted

Lucy: *late twenties; harassed mother of three young children; often left on her own.*
Rosemary: *lives next door to Lucy; could be much the same age but described as 'frail and mousey-looking'.*
Terry: *Rosemary's husband, 'a rather pudgy man in shirt sleeves'.*

A few easy chairs, and perhaps a coffee table, with several children's toys scattered around would suffice to suggest the living room.

Mother Figure

(*Lucy's sitting-room.*
It is a suburban room, fairly untidy, with evidence of small children. There are two doors—one to the kitchen and back door, one to the bedrooms and front door.
Lucy *hurries in from the bedrooms on her way to the kitchen. She is untidy, unmade-up, in dressing-gown and slippers.*)

Lucy (*calling behind her*) Nicholas! Stay in your own bed and leave Sarah alone.
(*The telephone rings.*
Lucy *goes out to the kitchen, returning at once with a glass of water.*)
All right, Jamie, darling. Mummy's coming with a dinkie . . . (*As she passes the telephone, she lifts the receiver off the rest and almost immediately replaces it.*) Mummy's coming, Jamie, Mummy's coming.
(**Lucy** *goes off to the bedrooms with the glass.*
The front door chimes sound. A pause, then they sound again
Lucy *returns from the bedrooms.*)
Sarah! You're a naughty, naughty girl. I told you not to play with Jamie's syrup. That's for Jamie's toothipegs . . .
(*The door chimes sound again.*
Lucy *ignores these and goes off to the kitchen. She returns almost at once with a toilet roll, hauling off handfuls of it as she goes to perform some giant mopping-up operation.*)
Nicholas, if you're not in your bed by the time I come up, I shall smack your botty.
(*There are two rings on the back door bell.*
Lucy *goes off to the bedroom.*
A pause.
Rosemary, *a rather frail, mousey-looking woman, comes in from the kitchen.*)

Rose. (*calling timidly*) Woo-hoo!
(**Lucy** *returns from the bedroom.*)

Lucy (*calling as before*) Now go to sleep. At once. (*seeing Rosemary*) Oh.

Rose. Hello. I thought you must be in.

Lucy (*puzzled*) Hello?

Rose. I thought you were in.

Lucy Yes.

Rose. You are.
Lucy Yes.
Rose. Hello.
Lucy Hello. (*A slight pause.*) Who are you?
Rose. Next door.
Lucy What?
Rose. From next door. Mrs Oates. Rosemary. Do you remember?
Lucy (*vaguely*) Oh, yes. Hello.
Rose. Hello. I did ring both bells but nobody seemed . . .
Lucy No. I don't take much notice of bells.
Rose. Oh.
Lucy I've rather got my hands full.
Rose. Oh yes. With the children, you mean? How are they?
Lucy Fine.
Rose. All well?
Lucy Yes.
Rose. Good. It's three you've got, isn't it?
Lucy Yes.
Rose. Still, I expect it's time well spent.
Lucy I haven't much option.
Rose. No.
Lucy Well.
Rose. Oh, don't let me—if you want to get on . . .
Lucy No.
Rose. I mean, if you were going to bed.
Lucy Bed?
Rose. (*indicating* **Lucy**'*s attire*) Well . . .
Lucy Oh, no. I didn't get dressed today, that's all.
Rose. Oh. Not ill?
Lucy No.
Rose. Oh.
Lucy I just wasn't going anywhere.
Rose. Oh, well . . .
Lucy I haven't been anywhere for weeks.
Rose. That's a shame.
Lucy I don't think I've got dressed for weeks, either.
Rose. Ah. No, well, I must say we haven't seen you. Not that we've been looking but we haven't seen you.
Lucy No. Do you want to sit down?
Rose. Oh, thank you. Just for a minute.
Lucy If you can find somewhere. (*She moves the odd toy.*)

Rose. (*sitting*) Yes, we were wondering if you were alright, actually. My husband and I—Terry, that's my husband—he was remarking that we hadn't seen you for a bit.

Lucy No.

Rose. We heard the children, of course. Not to complain of, mind you, but we heard them but we didn't see you.

Lucy No. (*She picks up various toys during the following and puts them in the play-pen.*)

Rose. Or your husband.

Lucy No.

Rose. But then I said to Terry, if they need us they've only to ask. They know where we are. If they want to keep themselves to themselves, that's all right by us. I mean, that's why they put up that great big fence so they could keep themselves to themselves. And that's all right by us.

Lucy Good.

Rose. And then ten minutes ago, we got this phone call.

Lucy Phone call?

Rose. Yes. Terry answered it—that's my husband—and they say will you accept a transfer charge call from a public phone box in Middlesbrough and Terry says, hallo, that's funny, he says, who do we know in Middlesbrough and I said, not a soul and he says, well, that's funny, Terry says, well who is it? How do we know we know him? If we don't know him, we don't want to waste money talking to him but if we do, it might be an emergency and we won't sleep a wink. And the operator says, well suit yourself, take it or leave it, it's all the same to me. So we took it and it was your husband.

Lucy Harry?

Rose. Harry, yes. Mr Compton.

Lucy What did he want?

Rose. Well—you. He was worried. He's been ringing you for days. He's had the line checked but there's been no reply.

Lucy Oh.

Rose. Has it not been ringing?

Lucy Possibly. I don't take much notice of bells. (*She goes to listen for the children.*)

Rose. Oh. Anyway, he sounded very worried. So I said I'd pop round and make sure. I took his number in case you wanted to . . . (*Lucy is clearly not listening.*)
Are you all right?

Lucy Yes, I was listening for Nicholas.
Rose. Oh. That's the baby?
Lucy No.
Rose. (*warmly*) Ah.
Lucy I'm sorry. I'm being very rude. It's just I haven't—spoken to anyone for days. My husband isn't home much.
Rose. Oh, I quite understand. Would you like his number?
Lucy What?
Rose. Your husband's telephone number in Middlesbrough. Would you like it? He said he'd hang on. It's from a hotel.
Lucy No.
Rose. Oh.
Lucy Whatever he has to say to me, he can say to my face or not at all.
Rose. Ah. (*laying a slip of paper gingerly on the coffee-table*) Well, it's there.
Lucy Would you care for a drink or something?
Rose. A drink? Oh—well—what's the time? Well—I don't know if I should. Half past—oh yes, well—why not? Yes, please. Why not? A little one.
Lucy Orange or lemon?
Rose. I beg your pardon?
Lucy Orange juice or lemon juice? Or you can have milk.
Rose. Oh, I see. I thought you meant . . .
Lucy Come on. Orange or lemon? I'm waiting.
Rose. Is there a possibility of some coffee?
Lucy No.
Rose. Oh.
Lucy It'll keep you awake. I'll get you an orange, it's better for you.
Rose. Oh . . .
Lucy (*as she goes*) Sit still. Don't run around. I won't be a minute.
(**Lucy** *goes out into the kitchen.*
Rosemary *sits nervously. She rises after a second, looks guiltily towards the kitchen and sits again. The door chimes sound.*
Rosemary *looks towards the kitchen. There is no sign of* **Lucy**. *The door chimes sound again.* **Rosemary** *gets up hesitantly.*)
Rose. (*calling*) Mrs—er . . .
Lucy (*off, in the kitchen*) Wait, wait, wait! I'm coming . . .
(*The door chimes sound again.*
Rosemary *runs off to the front door.* **Lucy** *returns from the kitchen with a glass of orange juice.*)
Here we are, Rosemary, I . . . (*She looks round the empty room, annoyed. Calling*) Rosemary! It's on the table.

(**Lucy** *puts the orange juice on the coffee-table and goes out to the kitchen again.* **Rosemary** *returns from the hall with* **Terry**, *a rather pudgy man in shirt sleeves.*)

Rose. (*sotto voce*) Come in a minute.

Terry I'm watching the telly.

Rose. Just for a minute.

Terry I wondered where you'd got to. I mean, all you had to do was give her the number . . .

Rose. I want you to meet her. See what you think. I don't think she's well.

Terry How do you mean?

Rose. She just seems . . .

Terry Is she ill?

Rose. I don't know . . .

Terry Well, either she's ill or she isn't.

Rose. Ssh.

(**Lucy** *returns from the kitchen with a plate of biscuits.*)

Lucy Here we are now. (*seeing* **Terry**) Oh.

Terry Evening.

Lucy Hello.

Rose. My husband.

Lucy Terry, isn't it?

Terry Yes.

Lucy That's a nice name, isn't it? (*pointing to the sofa*) Sit down there then. Have you got your orange juice, Rosemary?

(**Terry** *sits.*)

Rose. Yes, thank you. (*She picks up the glass of orange juice and sits.*)

Terry Orange juice?

Rose. Yes.

Terry What are you doing drinking that?

Rose. I like orange juice.

Lucy Now, here's some very special choccy bics but you mustn't eat them all. I'm going to trust you. (*She starts tidying up again.*)

Rose. (*still humouring her*) Lovely. (*She mouths 'say something' to* **Terry**.)

Terry Yes. Well, how are you keeping then—er, sorry, I'm forgetting. Lesley, isn't it?

Lucy Mrs Compton.

Terry Yes. Mrs Compton. How are you?

Lucy I'm very well, thank you, Terry. Nice of you to ask.

Terry And what about Har—Mr Compton?

Lucy Very well. When I last saw him. Rosemary dear, try not to make all that noise when you drink.

Rose. Sorry.

Terry Yes, we were saying that your husband's job obviously takes him round and about a lot.

Lucy Yes. (*She starts folding nappies.*)

Terry Doesn't get home as much as he'd like, I expect.

Lucy I've no idea.

Terry But then it takes all sorts. Take me, I'm home on the nose six o'clock every night. That's the way she wants it. Who am I . . .? (*Pause.*) Yes, I think I could quite envy your husband, sometimes. Getting about a bit. I mean, when you think about it, it's more natural. For a man. His natural way of life. Right back to the primitive. Woman stays in the cave, man the hunter goes off roving at will. Mind you, I think the idea originally was he went off hunting for food. Different sort of game these days, eh?

Rose. (*hissing*) Terry!

Terry Be after something quite different these days, eh? (*He nods and winks.*)

Lucy Now don't get silly, Terry.

Terry What? Ah—beg your pardon.

(*A pause.* **Terry** *munches a biscuit.* **Rosemary** *sips her orange juice.*)

Rose. Very pleasant orange juice.

Lucy Full of vitamin C.

Terry No, I didn't want to give you the wrong impression there. But seriously, I was saying to Rosie here, you can't put a man in a cage. You try to do that, you've lost him. See my point?

Lucy That can apply to women, too, surely?

Rose. Yes, quite right.

Terry What do you mean, quite right?

Rose. Well . . .

Terry You're happy enough at home, aren't you?

Rose. Yes, but—yes—but . . .

Terry Well then, that's what I'm saying. You're the woman, you're happy enough at home looking after that. I'm the man. I have to be out and about.

Rose. I don't know about that. You'd never go out at all unless I pushed you.

Terry What do you mean? I'm out all day.

Rose. Only because you have to be. You wouldn't be if you didn't have to be. When you don't, you come in, sit down, watch the television and go to bed.

Terry I have to relax.

Rose. You're always relaxing.

Terry Don't deny me relaxing.

Rose. I don't.

Terry Yes, you do, you just said . . .

Lucy Now, don't quarrel. I won't have any quarrelling.

Terry Eh?

Rose. Sorry.

Lucy Would you like an orange drink as well, Terry? Is that what it is?

Terry Er . . . Oh no—I don't go in for that sort of drink much, if you know what I mean. (*He winks, then reaches for a biscuit.*) I'll have another one of these though, if you don't mind?

Lucy Just a minute, how many have you had?

Terry This is my second. It's only my second.

Lucy Well, that's all. No more after that. I'll get you some milk. You better have something that's good for you.

Terry (*half rising*) Oh no—thank you, not milk, no.

Lucy (*going to the kitchen*) Wait there. (*seeing* **Terry** *has half risen*) And don't jump about while you're eating, Terry.

(**Lucy** *goes out to the kitchen.*)

Terry You're right. She's odd.

Rose. I said she was.

Terry No wonder he's gone off.

Rose. Perhaps that's why she's odd.

Terry Why?

Rose. Because he's gone off.

Terry Rubbish. And we'll have less of that, too, if you don't mind.

Rose. What?

Terry All this business about me never going out of the house.

Rose. It's true.

Terry It's not true and it makes me out to be some bloody idle loafer.

Rose. All I said . . .

Terry And even if it is true, you have no business saying it in front of other people.

Rose. Oh, honestly, Terry, you're so touchy. I can't say a thing right these days, can I?

Terry Very little. Now you come to mention it.

Rose. Niggle, niggle, niggle. You keep on at me the whole time. I'm frightened to open my mouth these days. I don't know what's got into you lately. You're in a filthy mood from the moment you get up till you go to bed . . .

Terry What are you talking about?

Rose. Grumbling and moaning . . .

Terry Oh, shut up.

Rose. You're a misery to live with these days, you really are.

Terry I said, shut up.

Rose. (*more quietly*) I wish to God you'd go off somewhere sometimes, I really do.

Terry Don't tempt me. I bloody feel like it occasionally, I can tell you.

Rose. (*tearfully*) Oh, lovely . . .

Terry If you think I enjoy spending night after night sitting looking at you . . . (*He throws the biscuit down.*) What am I eating these damn things for . . . you're mistaken. (*Thirsty from the biscuits, he grabs her orange juice glass and drains it in one.*)

Rose. That's mine, do you mind. (*She rises and stamps her foot.*)

Terry Come on. Let's go. (*He jumps up.*)

Rose. That was my orange juice when you've quite finished.
(**Lucy** *enters with a glass of milk.*)

Lucy Now what are you doing jumping about?
(**Rosemary** *sits.*)

Terry We've got to be going, I'm sorry.

Lucy Not till you've finished. Sit down.

Terry Listen. I'm sorry we . . .

Lucy (*seeing* **Rosemary***'s distraught state*) What's the matter with Rosemary?

Rose. (*sniffing*) Nothing . . .

Terry Nothing.

Lucy What have you been doing to her?

Terry Nothing.

Lucy Here's your milk.

Terry Thank you.

Lucy You don't deserve it.

Terry I don't want it.

Lucy Don't be tiresome.

Terry I hate the damned stuff.

Lucy I'm not going to waste my breath arguing with you, Terry. It's entirely up to you if you don't want to be big and strong.

Terry Now, look . . .

Lucy If you want to be a little weakling, that's up to you. Just don't come whining to me when all your nails and teeth fall out. Now then, Rosemary, let's see to you. (*She puts down the milk and picks up the biscuits.*) Would you like a choccy biccy?

Rose. No, thank you.
Lucy Come on, they're lovely choccy, look. Milk choccy . . .
Rose. No, honestly.
Terry Rosie, are you coming or not?
Lucy Well, have a drink, then. Blow your nose and have a drink, that's a good girl. (*seeing the glass*) Oh, it's all gone. You've drunk that quickly, haven't you?
Rose. I didn't drink it. He did.
Lucy What?
Rose. He drank it.
Lucy Terry, did you drink her orange juice?
Terry Look, there's a programme I want to watch . . .
Lucy Did you drink Rosemary's orange juice?
Terry Look, good night . . .
Rose. Yes, he did.
Lucy Well, I think that's really mean.
Rose. He just takes anything he wants.
Lucy Really mean.
Rose. Never thinks of asking.
Terry I'm going.
Lucy Not before you've apologized to Rosemary.
Terry Good night.
(**Terry** *goes out.*)
Lucy (*calling after him*) And don't you dare come back until you're ready to apologize. (*To* **Rosemary**) Never mind him. Let him go. He'll be back.
Rose. That's the way to talk to him.
Lucy What?
Rose. That's the way he ought to be talked to more often.
Lucy I'm sorry. I won't have that sort of behaviour. Not from anyone.
Rose. He'll sulk now. For days.
Lucy Well, let him. It doesn't worry us, does it?
Rose. No. It's just sometimes—things get on top of you—and then he comes back at night—and he starts on at me and I . . . (*She cries.*) Oh dear—I'm so sorry—I didn't mean to . . .
Lucy (*cooing*) Come on now. Come on . . .
Rose. I've never done this. I'm sorry . . .
Lucy That's all right. There, there.
Rose. I'm sorry. (*She continues to weep.*)
Lucy Look who's watching you.
Rose. Who?

Lucy (*picking up a doll*) Mr Poddle. Mr Poddle's watching you. (*She holds up the doll.*) You don't want Mr Poddle to see you crying, do you? Do you?

Rose. (*lamely*) No . . .

Lucy Do we, Mr Poddle? (*She shakes Mr Poddle's head.*) No, he says, no. Stop crying, Rosie. (*She nods Mr Poddle's head.*) Stop crying, Rosie. Yes—yes.

(**Rosemary** *gives an embarrassed giggle.*)

That's better. Was that a little laugh, Mr Poddle? Was that a little laugh?

(**Lucy** *wiggles Mr Poddle about, bringing him up to* **Rosemary**'*s face and taking him away again.*)

Was that a little laugh? Was that a little laugh? Was that a little laugh?

(**Rosemary** *giggles uncontrollably.*

Terry *enters from the hall and stands amazed.*)

Terry Er . . .

(**Lucy** *and* **Rosemary** *become aware of him.*)

Er—I've locked myself out.

Lucy Have you come back to apologize?

Terry You got the key, Rosie?

Rose. Yes.

Terry Let's have it then.

Lucy Not until you apologize.

Terry Look, I'm not apologizing to anyone. I just want the key. To get back into my own house, if you don't mind. Now, come on.

Rose. (*producing the key from her bag*) Here.

Lucy Rosemary, don't you dare give it to him.

Terry Eh?

Rose. What?

Lucy Not until he apologizes.

Terry Rosie, give me the key.

Lucy No, Rosemary. I'll take it. Give it to me.

Terry Rosie.

Lucy Rosemary.

Rose. (*torn*) Er . . .

Lucy (*very fiercely*) Rosemary, will you give me that key at once.

(**Rosemary** *gives* **Lucy** *the key*. **Terry** *regards* **Lucy**.)

Terry Would you mind most awfully giving me the key to my own front door?

Lucy Certainly.

Terry Thank you so much.

Lucy Just as soon as you've apologized to Rosemary.
Terry I've said, I'm not apologizing to anyone.
Lucy Then you're not having the key.
Terry Now listen, I've got a day's work to do tomorrow. I'm damned if I'm going to start playing games with some frustrated nutter . . .
Rose. Terry . . .
Lucy Take no notice of him, Rosemary, he's just showing off.
Terry Are you going to give me that key or not?
Lucy Not until you apologize.
Terry All right. I'll have to come and take it off you, won't I?
Lucy You try. You just dare try, my boy.
Terry All right. (*He moves towards* **Lucy**.)
Rose. Terry . . .
Lucy Just you try and see what happens.
Terry (*halted by her tone; uncertainly*) I'm not joking.
Lucy Neither am I.
Terry Look, I don't want to . . . Just give me the key, there's a good . . .
Lucy Not until you apologize to Rosemary.
Terry Oh, for the love of . . . All right (*To* **Rosemary**) Sorry.
Lucy Say it nicely.
Terry I'm very sorry, Rosie. Now give us the key, for God's sake.
Lucy When you've drunk your milk. Sit down and drink your milk.
Terry Oh, blimey . . . (*He sits.*)
Lucy That's better.
Terry I hate milk.
Lucy Drink it up.
(**Terry** *scowls and picks up the glass.* **Rosemary**, *unseen by* **Lucy**, *sticks her tongue out at him.* **Terry** *bangs down his glass and moves as if to hit her.*)
Terry!
Terry She stuck her tongue out at me.
Lucy Sit still.
Terry But she . . .
Lucy Sit!
(**Terry** *sits scowling.* **Rosemary** *smirks at him smugly.*)
(*seeing her*) And don't do that, Rosemary. If the wind changes, you'll get stuck like it. And sit up straight and don't slouch.
(**Rosemary** *does so.*)
Terry (*taking a sip of the milk*) This is horrible.
(*Silence. He takes another sip.*)

It's warm.
(*Silence. Another sip.*)

Terry There's a football international on television, you know.

Lucy Not until you've drunk that up, there isn't. Come on, Rosemary. Help Terry to drink it. 'Georgie Porgie Pudding and Pie, Kissed the girls and . . . ?'

Rose. '. . . made them cry.'

Lucy Good.

Rose.
Lucy } (*speaking together*) 'When the boys came out to play, Georgie Porgie ran away.'

Terry (*finishing his glass with a giant swallow*) All gone. (*He wipes his mouth.*)

Lucy Good boy.

Terry Can I have the key now, please?

Lucy Here you are.
(**Terry** *goes to take it.*)
What do you say?

Terry Thank you.

Lucy All right. Off you go, both of you.

Rose. (*kissing her on the cheek*) Night night.

Lucy Night night, dear. Night night, Terry.

Terry (*kissing* **Lucy** *likewise*) Night night.

Lucy Sleep tight.

Terry Hope the bugs don't bite.

Lucy Hold Rosemary's hand, Terry.
(**Rosemary** *and* **Terry** *hold hands.*)
See her home safely.

Terry Night.

Rose. Night.

Lucy Night night.
(**Terry** *and* **Rosemary** *go off hand in hand.*
Lucy *blows kisses.*
With a sigh.) Blooming kids. Honestly.
(*The telephone rings.* **Lucy**, *as she passes it, picks it up and replaces it as before. As she does so, the lights* **fade**.)

Points for discussion or written work

1. How is this sketch, in a sense, a response to the character in 'A Many Splendoured Thing' who said that marriage was 'not all love and kisses'?

2. Find as many signs of stress in Lucy as you can, not only in what she says, but in her dress, appearance and behaviour. Why do you think she is in this state?

3. What has happened between Lucy and her husband? Why does Lucy ignore his telephone calls? Do you think any blame ought to be attached to Harry for Lucy's behaviour, or is it her own fault?

4. We find Lucy's treatment of Rosemary and Terry very amusing; but what might be Ayckbourn's serious message behind the laughter he creates?

5. In reacting to Lucy's strange behaviour, what do Terry and Rosemary reveal about their own marriage and relationship with each other? Do they see each other in a new light after this experience?

6. Should neighbours 'keep themselves to themselves' or was Rosemary right in going round to see Lucy?

7. Could Terry and Rosemary have given Lucy better help? How?

8. What are the problems of young mothers at home, and how can they help themselves, or be helped to overcome them?

9. Imagine you are Lucy. Write a letter to a friend telling her about your family (use as much information from the extract as you can). Then go on to write about your worries and problems.

Suggestions for script or improvisation

1. Improvise or script a telephone conversation between Rosemary and/or Terry and Lucy's husband, Harry, in his hotel in Middlesbrough, after they have visited Lucy.

2. Improvise or script the scene where Harry returns home unexpectedly to find out what has happened to Lucy and why she has been ignoring his phone calls.

Moving on from there . . .

3. Imagine a young married couple: Nick and Jackie Cooper. Nick has an exciting and interesting job in an advertising agency, but Jackie is left at home with the children. She is lonely and has recently been telephoning her mother who lives several hundred miles away, during the day. They have just received a very large telephone bill. Script or improvise the conversation which follows. Nick does not know about Jackie's phone calls . . . you decide what happens.

4. Script or improvise a scene where a married couple, Steve and Jill Stevens, receive a letter from Jill's widowed father, asking them if he can come and stay. Jill used to be very close to her father before her marriage to Steve. But she realises that Steve and her father just do not get on. You can decide what happens . . . but Jill *does* feel that her father should be invited to stay, and that Steve should make more of an effort to be nice to him.

John Hopkins

Talking to a Stranger

The playwright John Hopkins, born in 1931, went to Cambridge University before joining the BBC, where he worked as a TV studio manager and later, producer. Not surprisingly, much of his output is written specially for television. He contributed over fifty episodes to the first series of '*Z*' *Cars* and since then has written many successful full-length television plays.

The play *Talking to a Stranger* is actually four plays linked by a common theme. They were first presented on BBC 2 on four successive Sunday evenings in October 1966 and were described by the *Observer* newspaper as 'the first authentic masterpiece written directly for television'. The four plays describe the events of one weekend involving four members of one family. Each play describes what happens from each individual's point of view, leading up to the tragic suicide of the mother. Together, they show how a family sometimes finds it hard to relate one to another, and how sometimes we subtly and subconsciously 'change' how we 'see' certain events, situations, and circumstances to suit our own prejudices, wishes and values.

The extract *The Innocent Must Suffer*, the final play of the quartet, is written from the mother's viewpoint. It explains why she was eventually driven to the desperate act of suicide. The family are just sitting down to tea. It is something of a special occasion because Terry, the daughter, does not often pay her parents a visit. Alan, the son, lives nearby with his wife Ellen and their two children. He tries to visit his parents as often as he can, but on this occasion has not brought his family. Alan has just broken the news that he has been offered a new job recently. Terry too has some news of her own, but as yet, only her mother guesses what it might be.

Characters: how it might be acted

Father: *aged seventy; tends to live in the past; prefers to avoid trouble if he can; sometimes a bit vague and forgetful, but still possesses 'the fragments of a bright, laughing personality'.*
Mother: *younger than father; tense and quite severe; finds it difficult to express her feelings and emotions. The 'noise' referred to was a television technique intended to convey her anxiety and her inner turmoil. Use acting to put this across.*
Alan: *aged 35; easy-going in some ways; a dutiful son, but his wife does not get on with his mother; might be described as being fairly ordinary and level-headed.*
Terry: *aged 30; 'attractive but not beautiful'; intelligent and independent; shares a flat with a friend, Jessica; has a sharp, sometimes sarcastic tongue.*

A table and some chairs would suggest the sitting room where the action takes place.

The Innocent Must Suffer

(*The front room. In the centre is a table, fully laid and adorned with cake and sandwiches, jelly and small cakes.* **Mother** *reaches for her chair.*)

Father (*from outside in the hall*) Alan. Terry. D'you hear?
Mother Ted. Come and sit down. (**Mother** *glances at the doorway as* **Father** *walks into the room.*)
Father Once they get talking . . .
Mother Here they come.
Father About time. (**Father** *turns to walk out into the hall again.*)
Mother Sit down. For goodness' sake!
(**Father** *turns and walks round the table to his chair,* **Terry** *and* **Alan** *walk into the room.*)
Alan What's all the shouting about?
Mother Sit down both of you.
Terry Are we expecting royalty?
Father What have you been talking about?
Terry (*looking at the table*) A feast—fit for a king. (*Pulls her chair back and sits down on it.*)

Alan Or queen—as the case may be!
Terry Right. You're right.
Father Terry?
(**Mother** *picks up the teapot and starts to pour out.*)
Mother Put your own sugar. Terry.
(**Terry** *reaches forward and picks up one of the cups. She passes it to her* **Father**.)
Father It's a long time since we've sat down, all of us together—and had tea.
Alan Yes, it is.
Terry Thought at least, we'd have the fatted calf.
Mother We didn't know you were coming, did we?
(**Terry** *picks up another cup and passes it to* **Alan**.)
Alan Thanks.
Father Feels like old times.
Terry Honestly, did we sit down to tea—like this? All of us. When we lived at home?
Mother Yes, of course we did.
Father What's this about a new job, Alan? What new job?
Alan It's by way of being promotion, as a matter of fact.
Father Promotion! That's good.
Mother It's about time.
Father They must be pleased with you.
Alan Yes, I think they are.
Father That's good. Isn't it, Mother? That's very good!
Mother Will it be more money?
Alan It would be. Really quite a lot more money.
Terry But you're not going to take it.
Alan Let's have the jam back. If you've finished with it?
(**Terry** *picks up the jam dish and holds it in her hands.*)
Terry (*carefully*) You're not going to take the job?
Alan I'm thinking about it. Jam?
(**Terry** *passes the jam dish to* **Alan**.)
(*politely*) Thanks.
Father You're not going to take it?
Alan I don't know.
Father They'll expect you to take it, won't they? If it's a promotion?
Alan What they expect and what they get—those are two very different things, Dad.
Terry Tara!
Mother Be quiet, Terry!

Father I don't understand, Alan. If it's a promotion and if it's more money, why aren't you going to take it?

Terry In a nutshell, Dad. That puts it in a sweet, crunchy nutshell. I can't wait to hear the answer.

Mother You listen to me, young lady. You're not too old . . .

Terry (*laughing*) To go across your knee? Oh, come on! Not too old—maybe—twice again too large.

Mother You can still be sent out of the room.

Terry (*harshly*) You send me out of the room, sweetie, you send me out of the house.

Father Don't speak to your mother like that.

Terry Goodness, is this my mother? I quite forgot. I thought it was my older sister. Lawks!

Mother You think you're very clever, don't you?

Terry Sometimes—yes. I think I get by.

Alan (*laughing*) In a fairly large crowd.

Father (*persistently*) Why aren't you going to take the job?

Alan Dad, look—I haven't decided what to do. Not yet.

Terry It means moving away from London?

(*Silence.*)

Alan Yes, it does.

Terry Lock, stock and barrel! If I can refer to darling Ellen . . .

Mother Is that what it means?

Alan Yes.

Mother You mustn't think about us, Alan.

(*The noise and the sound of her own words reverberates in* **Mother**'*s mind.*)

Your father and I can manage quite well. We've got the house. We've got enough money. The only thing that matters—really—is your career.

(*The words are distorted, almost obliterated by the noise.*)

We've tried to give you every possible chance, if this is the right thing for you to do—well, then—you must do it. That's all there is to it.

(*The noise scrambles the words.*)

After all, we're getting on now . . .

Terry Mrs Stephens, wife and mother . . .

(**Mother** *stares at* **Terry**'*s mouth opening and shutting, hardly able to distinguish the words.*)

. . . I present you with the Jesus of Nazareth award for suffering humanity. May God bless you and all who sail . . .

(**Mother** *slaps* **Terry** *hard across the face. Silence.*)

Mother You have a filthy mouth.

Terry (*gasping*) I'd better go and wash it.

(**Mother** *presses her hand to her forehead.*)

Mother How dare you speak like that in this house!

(**Father** *pushes back his chair and stands up.*)

Oh, yes. That's right!

Terry What—pray tell me, mother dear—is so special about this house?

(**Father** *walks round the table and* **Mother** *watches him. He walks behind* **Alan**, *who half-rises to speak to him.*)

Mother I might've known . . .

(**Father** *keeps as far as possible away from* **Mother**.)

Terry You think he is here? You think he is going to be offended, because your daughter . . .

Mother (*to* **Father** *viciously*) Coward!

Terry Why doesn't he strike me dead?

(**Mother** *turns her head and looks at* **Terry**.)

Mother I will not have you making your cheap jokes . . .

Terry If they're so shocking, why doesn't he reach down—pow!—and strike me dead?

(**Father** *opens the door of the room and walks out into the hall.*)

Mother You think you're so important?

Terry I think anyone, who needs—something—I don't know—anything. God knows . . .

Mother Your friends think that's funny, I suppose.

Terry Once and for all, the friends I've got—I haven't got any—you could butter on that piece of bread, eat and you still wouldn't choke on them.

Alan Terry, be quiet.

Terry Sweetie, I've only just got started.

Mother You don't make me laugh.

Terry Five elephants and a camel, stuck in a phone box, wouldn't make you laugh.

Mother If you can't control your tongue . . .

Terry You wouldn't let him take that job . . .

Mother . . . I think it's better, if you don't come and see us any more.

Alan Mother, no.

(*The front doorbell rings.*)

Mother Answer the door.

Alan Both of you . . .

Terry Truce.

(**Alan** *turns and walks across to the door. He goes out.*)

Mother Don't come and see us again.
Terry I won't.
(*Silence.* **Mother** *begins to clear the table. Automatically,* **Terry** *helps her.*)
Mother I can manage.
(**Terry** *puts the plate down and turns away from the table.*)
Terry I'll give you the address. In case you need—er—in case anything happens and you want to get in touch.
Mother Thank you.
Terry I'm on the phone.
Mother You might as well leave the number.
Terry I thought I would.
Mother When is it due?
Terry Four—five months.
Mother You ought to have a doctor look at you.
Terry I go to the hospital.
Mother Hmm.
Terry They're very good. I'm going to have it in hospital.
Mother They'll make you. If it's the first. (**Mother** *looks round at* **Terry**.) It is the first?
Terry First I've had. Yes.
Mother If you're anything like me, you'll have a rough time.
Terry That—seems to be the general opinion.
(*Silence.*)
Mother Do you want to have it?
Terry Yes.
Mother I didn't really—mean . . . (*She shrugs.*) If you want to come and see us . . .
Terry You meant it. Anyway I don't want to. I've only got five months—at the most—five. I have to learn a great many things. Looking after myself—living on my own . . .
Mother I thought you said—er—Jessica. Isn't that her name? Isn't she living with you?
Terry For the moment. Yes. Just—for the moment.
Mother Till—the baby?
Terry No.
(*Silence.*)
Mother Do you want me to tell your father?
Terry You do what you want to do.
Mother No. It's up to you.
Terry I'd rather—rather you didn't—if that's possible?
(**Mother** *nods her head.*)

Mother You'll drop us a line.

Terry Not—not for a while.

Mother When . . .

(*The chime of an ice-cream van tinkles outside in the street.*)

Mother Oh, I must get . . . (**Mother** *stops and shrugs.*) No need. No, I don't have to get any ice cream. Have you thought about—all the things? You'll need a great many . . .

Terry I've thought. I've read. I've asked.

Mother You've—told a lot of people?

Terry No one. It isn't something . . . (**Terry** *shrugs.*) Anyway, I have to go on working. No—a few theoretical . . .

Mother I always thought . . .

(*Silence.*)

Terry I'm really very frightened.

Mother There's no need.

(**Alan** *walks back into the room.*)

Terry I'll go and say good-bye to Dad.

(**Terry** *walks out of the room.* **Alan** *walks across and shuts the door. He turns and looks at his* **Mother**.)

Alan She is pregnant.

Mother Hmm. (**Mother** *walks across to the window.*)

Alan Makes a difference.

Mother What?

Alan She isn't—you know—responsible . . .

Mother For what she says?

Alan She doesn't mean . . . (**Alan** *walks towards his* **Mother**.) She never did—half the things she says . . .

Mother She can be very hurtful.

Alan She doesn't think.

Mother Stands at this window—hours at a time.

Alan Dad? (**Alan** *stands beside his* **Mother**.)

Mother Looks out. I think . . . (*She turns and looks at* **Alan**.) You're going to take the job?

Alan I don't know.

Mother You're going to take it. (**Mother** *walks past him to the table, and continues clearing the tea things.*)

Alan (*quietly*) I haven't made up my mind.

Mother You might have told me about it.

Alan I haven't known myself . . .

Mother 'Stead of—blurting it . . . (**Mother** *stops speaking and stares down at the table.*)

Alan What's the matter? (**Alan** *walks across to his* **Mother**.)

Mother You might have told me.
(*Silence.*)
Talked it over . . .
Alan I was going to.
Mother When are you going?
Alan I don't know—if . . .
Mother When?
Alan Soon.
Mother Where?
Alan (*abruptly*) Australia.
Mother How long have you known?
Alan Not long.
Mother How long? Long enough to phone? Long enough . . .
Alan I didn't want to tell you on the phone.
Mother Didn't want to tell me. Frightened . . .
Alan Oh, for . . .
Mother . . . to tell me.
Alan . . . pity's sake!
Mother Talked it over with Ellen?
Alan Yes.
Mother She wants to go.
Alan Can we—look—if we're going to talk—you know—leave Ellen . . .
Mother Found time to talk about it—to Ellen?
Alan Leave her out of it!
Mother Tom Rutherford. You remember Tom?
Alan What?
Mother He went to Canada. D'you remember him?
Alan No. Yes. I think so. I don't honestly . . .
Mother You went to the same school. He was round here . . .
Alan All right! I remember him. What about—Tom Rutherford?
Mother He went to Canada. He took his mother and father with him.
Alan You want to go to Australia?
Mother I'm not saying . . .
Alan Just—some people—children—know how to behave?
Mother Paid for everything.
Alan Is he married? Does he have children?
Mother Yes. He's married.
Alan Children?
Mother I don't know.
Alan His wife—gets on with his mother? Put them in the same room . . .

Mother It isn't every woman . . .
Alan . . . they won't scratch each other's eyes out?
Mother The way Ellen treats me . . .
Alan The way you treat Ellen . . .
Mother Since the day you got married . . .
Alan (*mocking her almost*) She's tried to take me away from you.
Mother It isn't funny!
Alan (*sarcastically*) She's tried to come between . . .
Mother You make a joke . . .
Alan (*harshly*) It is a joke!
Mother She's never tried . . .
Alan She breaks her heart—trying!
Mother She never comes to see me. She never even phones me.
Alan Why? Have you thought? I mean, what happens when she phones?
Mother Of course, you take her side.
Alan What do you say to her?
Mother You've always taken her side.
Alan She's my wife. I love her.
Mother You're supposed—to . . .
(*Silence.*)
I'm your mother.

Points for discussion or writing

1. Re-read the character descriptions given earlier. From this short extract, do you think they are accurate? Can you identify each character's personality from what happens here?

2. How do Father, Mother and Terry each react to Alan's news that he has been offered promotion? Why did each react differently?

3. Does Terry enjoy a closer relationship with her father or her mother? How is this shown?

3. Why does Mother call Father 'a coward'?

5. What might be the reasons behind Terry's unpleasantness to her mother? Is Mother too hard on Terry? Do they change when they are left alone, and if so, why?

6. John Hopkins, in describing Terry elsewhere in the play, writes that her eyes occasionally 'open shafts of darkness'. What might he mean by this?

7. What do we learn here about Alan's relationship with his mother? Had his marriage to Ellen altered things between them? Was Alan's mother jealous of his wife? Is this unusual?

Suggestions for script or improvisation

1. Improvise or script the scene where Mother is alone with Father, after Terry and Alan have left. She decides to tell him that Terry is pregnant. How will he react?

2. Improvise or script a scene with Alan and his wife Ellen coming to Alan's parents' house to discuss their move to Australia. Each character feels differently about the situation. Alan would like to keep everyone happy, and tries to keep the peace. His mother would like to emigrate with Alan, but his father wants to stay at home in England now that he knows Terry is pregnant. Ellen is against them going, saying at their age such a long journey would be out of the question, but knowing secretly that she could never endure

Alan's mother's company for long. You decide what happens when they begin to talk it out.

Going on from there . . .

3. Write or improvise a family meal. Include the same number of characters as in the extract, but make the children your age (no younger). One of them wants to go on an expensive ski-ing holiday with his/her school. They are talking about this when father returns home from work. He has just learnt that day that he is to be made redundant in less than a month. He must eventually break this news to his family, but finds it difficult at first.

4. Write or improvise a scene between a Father/Mother and Son/Daughter, where the latter has eventually to tell the parent that he/she wants to leave home. Remember to create convincing detail and good reasons why he/she feels this way. You may decide yourself on the exact age of the Son/Daughter, bearing in mind that this will affect the improvisation greatly.

School

How often have you heard the expression that 'schooldays are the happiest days of your life!' Do you agree? Do you think that after you have left, you will look back on your time in school with affection?

These two extracts look at aspects of life in two different schools. Are they anything like your own? Look at the two pictures and, from what you can see and deduce from them, use them as a basis for improvising the sort of lesson you could expect from each teacher. How would a class react to each teacher; how would its behaviour differ with each teacher? Which teacher would you prefer, and why?

Barry Hines and Allan Stronach

Kes

The playwrights Barry Hines was born in 1939 near Barnsley, Yorkshire. His greatest interest at school was football, and on leaving, Hines joined Barnsley, playing mainly in their 'A' team, while working at various jobs from apprentice mining surveyor to blacksmith's assistant. Later he trained to be a teacher and taught P.E. for two years in a London comprehensive. His first novel, *The Blinder*, was published in 1966, followed by the more successful *Kestrel for a Knave* in 1968. This was made into a highly-acclaimed film, and then, with Allan Stronach, into a play which was first performed in a Sheffield school in 1974.

The play *Kes* is the story of Billy Casper and his relationship with a kestrel which he finds and trains. It is a moving tale of Billy's loneliness, his isolation from friends at school and from his family at home, and how he overcomes this when he becomes interested and involved with his 'Kes'.

The extract As a teacher, Hines provides some closely observed moments from school life. Here Billy Casper, who has been caught being inattentive in morning assembly, is waiting outside the Headmaster Mr Gryce's office. Together with him are Macdowall, who is accused of coughing in assembly, and three others who had been caught smoking the day before.

Characters: how it might be acted

Mr Gryce: *described in the book as 'like a bulldog', an angry, intolerant man.*

Macdowall: *aged about 14; a bully; does not like teachers, and they don't much like him; always in trouble at school.*

Billy: *aged 14, but small for his years; something of a 'loner'; sometimes bullied in school.*

Three Smokers: *assorted boys of the same age; probably disreputable.*

Messenger: *younger, rather timid boy; innocent of any wrongdoing.*

All these characters have a northern accent.
A table and chair would suggest the Headmaster's office.

Kes

(*The* **Three Smokers**, **Billy** *and* **Macdowall** *are waiting for the Headmaster to return.*)

Macdow. It wasn't me that coughed you know. I'm going to tell Gryce that an' all.

1st S. It makes no difference whether you tell him or not, he doesn't listen.

Macdow. I'll bring my father up if he gives me the stick anyway.

Billy What you always bringing your father up for? He never does anything when he comes. They say last time he came up, Gryce gave him stick as well.

Macdow. At least I've got a proper father to bring up, that's more than you can say Casper.

Billy Shut your gob, Macdowall.

Macdow. Why, what you going to do about it?

Billy You'd be surprised.

Macdow. Right then, I'll see you at break.

Billy Anytime you want.

Macdow. Right then.

Billy Right.

(*Pause. A* **Small Boy** *enters with a message for Gryce.*)

1st S. If you've come for the stick you'd better get to the back of the queue.

Mess. I've not come for the stick; Crossley's sent me with a message.

(*Pause.*)

Macdow. It's his favourite trick this. He likes to keep you waiting. He thinks it makes it worse.

2nd S. (*takes cigarettes etc. out of his pocket and goes to the* **boy**) Here, you'd better save us these until after. If he searches us he'll only take them off us and give us another two strokes.

Mess. I don't want them, you're not getting me into trouble as well.

2nd S. Who's getting you into trouble. You can give them back after.

Mess. (*shaking head*) Don't want them.

2nd S. Do you want some fist instead?

(**The Three Smokers** *surround him and fill his pockets with cigarettes, lighters etc.*)

Billy Hey! He's here. Gryce Pudding.
(**Gryce** *enters.* **Boys** *stand in a line.*)

Gryce Right you reprobates. (*They go in.*) The same old faces. Why is it always the same old faces?

Mess. Please sir.

Gryce Don't interrupt boy, when I'm speaking. (*He walks down the line.*) I'm sick of you boys, you'll be the death of me. Not a day goes by without me having to see a line of boys. I can't remember a day—not one day—in all the years that I've been in this school, and how long's that? . . . ten years, and the school is no better now than it was on the day it opened. I can't understand it. I really can't. (*He goes to the window and admires the neatly cut lawns outside. He remains there as he continues talking.*) I thought I understood young people. I should be able to with all my experience—I've taught in this city thirty-five years now—but there's something happening today that's frightening. It makes me feel that it's all been a waste of time. (**The Boys** *look at each other, bored.*) Like it's a waste of time talking to you boys now, because you're not taking a blind bit of notice of what I'm saying. I know what you're thinking now, you're thinking why doesn't he shut up and get on with it. That's what you're thinking isn't it? Isn't it Macdowall?

Macdow. No sir.

Gryce Of course it is. I can see it in your eyes lad, they're glazed over.

Mess. Please sir.

Gryce Shut up lad. As far as I can see there's been no advance at all in discipline, decency, manners or morals. And do you know how I know this? Because I still have to use this every day. (*He takes the cane from the top of his desk.*) I can understand why we had to use it back in the twenties and thirties. Those were hard times, they bred hard people and it needed hard measures to deal with them. We knew where we stood in those days; they bred people with respect for a start. Even today a man will stop me in the street and say—'Hello Mr Gryce, remember me?' And we'll pass away the time of day and he'll laugh about the thrashings I used to give him. (**The Boys** *have stopped listening altogether by now.*) They took it then, but not now. Not in this day of the common man, when every boy quotes his rights and shoots off home for his father as soon as I look at him . . No guts . . . no backbone . . . you've nothing to commend you whatsoever. (*He swishes the stick in front of them.*) So for want of a better solution

I continue using the cane, knowing full well that you'll be back time and time again for some more. You smokers will carry on smoking just the same. (**One of the smokers** *is smirking at the other boys.*) Yes you can smirk lad. I bet your pockets are ladened up in readiness for break this very moment, aren't they? Aren't they? Well just empty them, come on, get your pockets emptied.

(**The Three Smokers, Billy** *and* **Macdowall** *begin to empty their pockets.*)

Mess. Please sir . . .

Gryce Quiet lad and get your pockets emptied. (*He moves along the line inspecting the contents distastefully.*) This can't be true, I don't believe it. (*He puts the stick back on the desk.*) Keep your hands out. (*He goes along the line again frisking their clothing. He finally comes to the* **young boy**.) Ah! Ah!

Mess. Please sir . . .

Gryce You're a regular little cigarette factory aren't you? (*He methodically takes the objects from the boy's pockets.*) You deceitful boy. You didn't think you could get away with a weak trick like that, did you? (*He puts all the objects into the basket.*) Right, one at a time, over here.

(**The Three Smokers, Billy, Macdowall** *and the* **Boy** *individually come to the headmaster's desk, lean over it and are given two strokes each. It is important that this is done as realistically as possible and it should certainly not be funny in any way at all.* **The Three Smokers, Billy** *and* **Macdowall**, *although it hurts them, take it in their stride. As Gryce has already suggested, they will probably be back for more on another occasion. When it is the* **Messenger's** *turn, however,* **Gryce** *has to direct him to the table and he leaves the room crying.*)

Points for discussion or written work

1. What sort of a teacher is Gryce? Try to build up a detailed description of him from what you see and hear of him here. (Remember for a complete picture of any character in a play, you must look at what other characters say about him and how they react to him, as well as what he says and does himself.)

2. What does Gryce's treatment of the messenger suggest about the way he deals with pupils in the rest of the school? Would Gryce make an effective headmaster? Justify your opinion.

3. Is corporal punishment—use of the cane—a fair way of punishing these boys? Do you think its use is ever justified? If you were Gryce, how would you have dealt with the situation here?

4. Do you think teachers are right in discouraging pupils from smoking in school? What would be the best way of going about this?

5. When Gryce suggests that 'there's been no advance at all in discipline, decency, manners or morals' what do you think he means? Would you agree with him?

6. Design a striking poster, aimed at people of your age, pointing out the damaging health consequences, and possible anti-social effects, of smoking.

7. Conduct a survey in your class or school of views for or against corporal punishment. Organise a formal debate with two speakers in favour and two opposing the motion, 'This House believes that corporal punishment should remain as an option for school discipline.'

Suggestions for script or improvisation

1. Improvise or script the scene where the messenger's parents visit the school to complain about Gryce's treatment of their son. Include the following characters: Gryce, Messenger, Parents, School Secretary. (Remember to give all unnamed characters convincing names.)

2. Improvise or script a staff meeting at Gryce's school, which has been called by him to discuss rumours of complaints by some staff about his use of the cane. Try to include both sides of the argument so that some staff support Gryce, some favour abandoning corporal punishment altogether, while some do not commit themselves at all. Both sides have to justify their views. How would Gryce react? It's up to you to decide.

Moving on from there . . .

3. Set up a scene in school where a Head Teacher has to interview a pupil who has been playing truant. You can decide what happens and why he/she has been missing lessons. You could also include the parents if you wanted to include more characters.

4. Use the following titles as starting points for plays or improvisations about school: 'New Boy'; 'The Bully'; 'The Outsider'; 'Incident in the Classroom'; 'Your Friends will be your Downfall'.

Barry Reckord

Skyvers

The playwright Barry Reckord is Jamaican and has written: *You in Your Small Corner* (1960), *Skyvers* (1963), *Don't Gas the Blacks* (1969), *Time to Love You* (1973) and *X* (1974). He was educated at Cambridge and for a time worked in British theatre before returning to Jamaica.

The play *Skyvers* is a realistic, if now slightly dated, portrait of life in a London comprehensive school. The five central characters are spending their last week in school before leaving. The play examines their attitude to school in the light of their experience, and indeed, the school's attitude to them. It raises some very important questions about the nature and quality of secondary education. *Skyvers* was first performed at The Royal Court Theatre, London on 23 July, 1963.

The extract A group of boys who are about to leave school are waiting in their classroom for the teacher of their first lesson to appear. As there is obviously some delay, they begin playing football in the room, using a school textbook as the ball. One of the boys, Adams, is on lookout at the door.

Characters: how it might be acted

Freeman: *a new teacher; youngish; finding it difficult to keep control.*
Cragge: *leader of the boys; rather boastful and full of himself; going out with a girl called Helen.*
Brook: *has also been seeing Helen. This is a source of tension between him and Cragge.*
Colman, Adams, Jordan: *other boys in the class; all are probably leaving school shortly; might be termed 'under achievers', but are not necessarily unintelligent.*
Headmaster: *traditional; a strict disciplinarian.*

Setting: simple—a school classroom. Try giving the boys London accents.

(**Cragge** *picks up a book and kicks it across the room.*)
Adams Head.
Jordan Saved.
(**Brook** *kicks wildly, misses and falls down; they all laugh at him.*)
Colman (*to* **Jordan**) Don't bloody push.
(*The noise goes on.*)
Brook Belt up.
Cragge Goal.
Adams (*hugging* **Cragge**) Beauty.
Colman The cover's come off.
Cragge Hide it in the desk.
Brook Another!
Jordan They'll start bloody missing 'em.
Brook (*kicks the book against the wall, throwing up his hands and smiling*) Score one like that tonight, Craggsie, and the girls will love you.
Adams (*on the lookout at the door*) That new bloke's comin'.
(*Enter* **Freeman**. *Dead silence.*)
Freeman What were you playing with?
Adams Playin'?
Freeman This book, wasn't it? (*He takes the ragged book off the floor.*)
Adams This book, sir (*producing a football boot*).
(*The boys laugh.*)
Freeman Then I suppose there's no point asking who did this?
Jordan We came in and found it there.
Brook (*insolently*) That's the truth.
Freeman (*quietly to* **Brook**) What's your name?
Brook What's yours?
Freeman (*ignoring the insolence*) Are there only five of you? What's happened to the rest of the class?
Adams Gone down the drain.
(*The others often glance at* **Brook** *for applause.*)
Colman Left, sir.
Jordan Left, left, right, left.
Freeman Be quiet you.
Adams The rest skidaddled the minute they touched fifteen.
Colman We're leaving.
Freeman So you leave when the term ends.
Adams Tell us a little about yourself, sir.
Jordan (*a low grumble*) What's 'appened to Barker?
(*Cries, led by* **Brook**, 'We want Barker! We want Barker!'

Cragge *keeps out of it.*)

Freeman (*gently*) Quiet boys . . . I said quiet . . . Mr Barker is away. I'll be teaching you for the next few days to the end of term.

Colman A few days! There's the whole soggin' week.

Freeman (*gaining a laugh*) Worse luck for me.

Adams Brooksie won't stay the week, I bet.

Brook I never 'ave been 'ere a whole week, since I been to this school.

Colman The worse lot in the school they've ever 'ad, they reckon us.

Freeman (*to the leader*, **Brook**) Why don't you stay on in school?

(*Jeers and catcalls.*)

Doesn't your father want you to stay on and learn more?

(*The boys laugh.*)

Voice More!

Brook (*to them*) Shut up. (*To* **Freeman**) Wot's my dad got to do with it? It's my life.

Freeman Doesn't anybody want to stay for the G.C.E.?

Cragge 'Ands up all who want to stay?

(*Everybody groans. No hands go up.*)

'Ands up.

(*No hands.*)

(*To* **Freeman**) Bashful, ain't they?

Colman No point in my stayin'.

Jordan 'E's got an apprenticeship.

Colman My dad's in the print and 'e's gettin' me in.

Freeman But you could stay on at school and learn. You don't have to be content with a trade.

Jordan I'm going into the docks, it's a skill and a privilege.

Freeman Privilege?

Jordan I got two uncles in. You got to 'ave your family in the docks to get in.

Freeman Don't any of you want to be educated?

Cragge Look at you—you're educated and where did it get you—teaching!

Adams What a life.

Brook You teach me to make dough and that's teaching.

Freeman So money is all that counts?

Adams (*quite sincere*) What else?

Jordan What's wrong with it?

Freeman (*with emphasis*) What's wrong with it!

Colman (*nasty, and resenting* **Freeman's** *attitude*) You tell us, you're the teacher!

Cragge Look at all them teachers with G.C.E. and more. They're forty before they can buy a car without worryin'. Look at you ridin' a push bike and teachin'.

Adams What a life.

Cragge Footballers drive a Cresta when they're twenty.

Brooke (*jeering at* **Cragge**) He's gonna be one of them.

Cragge (*to* **Brook**) Yeah, and we'll see who the crowd follow then. (*To* **Freeman**) Look at Cliff Richard, Johnny Haynes, Helen Shapiro. D'you think they're educated. But they're the names ain't they. They make the news.

Freeman What are you going to do?

Cragge Who me?

Freeman Yes, what job are you going into?

Adams 'E 'asn't got a job. 'E'll be labourin'.

Cragge I ain't much good with me 'ands.

Freeman But you don't want to stay on at school.

Brook Get this thickie: they don't teach nothing that's any good to us.

Freeman (*to* **Cragge**) So what are you going to do?

Colman Don't say we got no ambition.

Brook (*to* **Colman**) I'll tell you what he's not going to do.

Colman What?

Brook Helen! 'E tried to muck about and she insulted him . . .

Cragg That's a lie.

Freeman What's this?

Adams So we want your name, sir, please, sir.

Freeman Freeman, that's my name. What's your name?

Adams Piggot. (**Adams** *is small.*) Lester Piggot.

Freeman Now you'll understand that without knowing your names I can't control the class, so I'll punish anybody who trumps up a name. (*Suddenly pointing to* **Adams**) You. What's your name?

Adams Smith, sir.

Freeman All right. Let's take some current topic that interests you and talk about it. Any topic.

Brook Girls.

Freeman Let's take the bomb, for instance.

Jordan Girls.

Freeman I suggest the bomb. Let's hear what you think of . . .

Colman Girls.

Adams Girls.

Brook And ask old Cragge about 'Elen.

All Girls! Girls!

Freeman Don't shout at me, please.

Voices We want girls.

Freeman (*taking up the challenge*) Right then, girls. You then, talk about girls.

Brook 'Is name is 'Elen.

(*The boys laugh at* **Cragge**.)

Freeman Start your talk.

Cragge Well, I don't go much for the young talent because it ain't very well informed see?

(*Laughter.*)

I like 'em thirty, thirty-five, even forty like; get a bit a lolly and a lot of fun out of 'em, see?

Freeman (*warningly*) Good clean fun, eh, lad? Because that's what we're supposed to be talking about.

Cragge But if you can't cop an amacher (amateur) like . . .

Freeman Let's hear about the mixed youth clubs you lads go to.

Cragge Not me. No youth for me. I told yer . . . Too easy . . . You dunno what you may catch.

Brook Easy wiv everyone except 'im . . .

Adams (*to* **Cragge**) As you was sayin' . . .

Cragge (*to* **Brooke**) Helen's an easy feel but a hard lay if you really wanna know.

Freeman (*violently*) Quiet!

Colman You asked 'im, didn't you?

Freeman (*to* **Cragge**) Sit down.

Cragge (*very excited*) If I can't find an amacher, I like the old pros, see, because you can . . .

(*He makes a suggestive gesture.*
Hell breaks loose.
Enter **Headmaster**.)

Head Just stand where you are. I heard the noise. Could you just tell me what happened, Mr Freeman?

Freeman (*aside, to the* **Head**, *in a strained voice as though he is on trial – the rest cannot hear*) I said we'd take some subject and discuss it, say the bomb, and they said, 'no, girls'. So I thought I'd better not shy away from the subject. Then this boy said he liked the old pros best because you can—and made a filthy gesture.

Head (*aside, to* **Freeman**) Really these boys need special handling, Mr Freeman, there's nothing much we can do! A few of them are on probation. (*Straightening his cane*) Come here, Cragge. Filthy gestures, eh? Bend over!

(**Cragge** *obeys.*)

(*To the whole class*) Girls . . . my mother was a girl. I have the deepest respect, indeed, reverence, for her . . . My sister was a girl too. (*To* **Adams**, *who is smiling*) Yes, you worm, if your filthy little mind would let you, you'd think of your mother when you think of girls. I do . . . Now, I have from time to time in my life, while I was going about my business, seen women standing at street corners. I have assumed who they were. But I have never in my life spoken to such a woman. And certainly none of *my* sons have ever spoken to such a woman. Neither have we ever spoken about them. At any rate whatever you talk about in the streets or even in your own homes, we leave the subject out of this school, right out. (*To* **Cragge**) Bend over, boy.

(*He whips* **Cragge** *who winces at the first stroke, and tries hard not to wince for the other five; then the* **Head** *says:*)

The subject Mr Freeman suggested you discuss was the bomb. You will stay in this classroom after school tomorrow night and write me an essay on war. I'll make you think.

Points for discussion or written work

1. Imagine you are a School Inspector, and that this extract from Freeman's lesson had been videotaped. What advice would you give him to improve his control of the class and the content of his lesson?

2. Do you think the Headmaster dealt with this situation effectively? When he said 'I'll make you think', what did he mean? Would he have been successful?

3. Are examinations the only reason for attending school, as Mr Freeman seems to think? or the only key to success? Can you suggest ways in which your own school, for example, prepares you for the outside adult world, apart from teaching you to pass exams?

4. Why were these boys so bored with school? Were they catered for adequately. Try to say what lessons and what kind of teachers they had? Would it have been better for them to have left school early? Could their time have been spent more profitably? If so, how?

5. Draw up a blank school timetable for your school week, leaving out the lessons you would *normally* have each day. Then fill in the timetable you feel would be most relevant and useful to these boys. It can include subjects not usually taught in schools and time which might be spent outside school. You might even want to alter radically the timing of the school day. Whatever option you choose, however, you must justify. Then try constructing the ideal timetable which would most suit you.

Suggestions for script or improvisation

1. Improvise or script the scene in the Headmaster's office later, when the Head sends for Freeman to discuss what happened in the lesson. The two men obviously differ in approach and attitude to these pupils and you must make this clear in the interview that takes place.

2. Improvise or script the scene in the staff room when Freeman returns after his disastrous lesson, and tells

other staff what happened. It can be made clear that the class he has just taken for the first time are always difficult. Try to include varying attitudes on the part of the staff to these pupils, from open hostility to guarded sympathy.

Moving on from there . . .

3. Situation: a boys'/girls' changing room after a P.E. lesson. One of the pupils is about to leave when he/she discovers that quite a large sum of money which had been left in his/her school bag is missing. How does the group of pupils, and their teacher, sort out this problem? Would pupils be searched, for example, or the police called in? You decide.

4. Script or improvise a scene between two anxious parents and the headmaster/mistress of a large urban comprehensive school. The parents are convinced that their son/daughter is being bullied in school. He/she may be brought in, if you wish; how would the child react to learning that the parents had made this known to the Head? Suspected bullies could also be interviewed.

The World of Work

Most of our life is spent sleeping, but, if we are fortunate enough to find employment, a good proportion of our time is spent working. These plays examine the 'world of work' from the business of actually finding employment to the importance of job satisfaction and Trades Unions in our working lives. Use the pictures as starting points for your own plays, improvisations or stories about the 'world of work'.

Peter Terson

Zigger Zagger

The playwright Peter Terson was born in Newcastle upon Tyne in 1932, and was brought up in a hard world of empty shipyards and dole queues. He left school at 15 and worked in a variety of jobs before spending two years in the R.A.F. After teacher-training, he taught P.E. for ten years, writing plays in his spare time and receiving, in his own words, 'many rejection slips' from publishers. Eventually, Peter Cheeseman at the Victoria Theatre, Stoke-on-Trent, accepted Terson's play *A Night to Make the Angels Weep*, and it was presented there in 1965. In the following year, Terson received an Arts Council grant to be Resident Playwright at Stoke. He began work on *Zigger Zagger* in that year, and since then has written several television plays including: *I'm In Charge of These Ruins, The Apprentices* and *Good Lads at Heart.*

The play Terson was specially commissioned to write *Zigger Zagger* for The National Youth Theatre by its Director, Michael Croft, in 1966. In writing the play, Terson followed a technique he had learnt at Stoke: of working with a director to produce a play that could be altered and varied during the actual rehearsals. *Zigger Zagger* is a lively and penetrating study of a football hooligan. The stage on which it was originally performed was even made to look like a football stadium, and the play itself is full of the sights, sounds, colour and excitement of a football match. A large cast of 'supporters' punctuate the play with choruses which, although sounding like familiar football chants, on further reflection, provide deeper comment on the action.

The extract This scene reflects what could happen to Cragge in *Skyvers* and pupils like him. Harry Philton, a school leaver, is being interviewed by a Youth Careers Officer. The scene starts quite realistically, but ends, somewhat unusually, with the Careers Officer singing a song. This technique, called alienation, distances the audience from the action and is supposed to encourage them to think more deeply about what is happening. A chorus of football supporters provides a further, final comment.

Characters: how it might be acted

Harry: *school leaver; described by his Headmaster in these terms, 'Left school when he was fifteen. Like the rest of them. He hadn't learnt much in the last year. Didn't want to. I put him on milk duty and biscuits. He was also ink monitor. Work and Attainment: Fair. Conduct: Fair. Appearance: Fair. He wasn't Britain's last hope, but you've got to be fair to the lad.'*
Youth Careers Officer: *no specified age; brisk at his job and somewhat easily annoyed.*
Football Supporters: *age and sex unspecified.*

The long speech at the end—originally written as a song—could be recited like a ballad or poem. The whole class could practice and perform the final chorus using the music hall song tune, *I'm Forever Blowing Bubbles.*
A table with two chairs would suggest the office of the Careers Officer.

Zigger Zagger

(*The Youth Careers Office.*
The **Youth Careers Officer** *in his cubicle.*)

Officer Next.
(*Enter* **Harry**.)
Come into my cubicle. Wait. Signed Arnold Baxter. I am the Youth Careers Officer. Now lad, come on, stand up straight, no slouching, what can I do for you?

Harry I want a job.

Officer Oh, just like that, eh? You want a job? Just like that? See all these cards? See them? That's youths wanting jobs. See this handful of cards here, that's jobs.

Harry Bad as that, is it? I'll go then.

Officer Oh no you don't! Do me out of a job, would you! Sit down. Card. Had a job before, have you?

Harry Yes.

Officer What was it?

Harry Paper round.

Officer Good. Good. Paper round is good for a youth. Did you get it through us?

Harry No. Through the papers. Situations Vacant columns.

Officer Oh, I see. I see. Situations Vacant. You got it through them? Newspaper columns with the second-hand bikes and the pets for Miscellaneous Sale. Why didn't you buy a piano while you were about it?

Harry Didn't want a piano.

Officer The government goes to all the fuss to build this lovely building, houses us, staffs it with qualified civil servants, we sit here with only two tea breaks a day waiting to serve the public, wanting to serve the public, willing to serve the public and yet you go and get a job through the newspaper columns. Like a lost budgie. But now you come whining to us.

Harry You must sit here waiting for a comedian's job to turn up.

Officer Now look, lad. I'm here to help. To serve the public. I'm here to find youths careers. That's why I'm called Youth Careers Officer. I took a course in it. University Sandwich. I was trained in social psychology. I was trained in adolescent problems. So now, button your lip, this is my cubicle. Now, you want a job. What certificates you got?

Harry Certificates?

Officer Mental certificates lad. Exams. G.C.E. C.S.E. D.D. Certificates. Qualifications.

Harry I've got me Bronze Medallion for Life Saving and me Tenderfoot in the Cubs.

Officer Is that all?

Harry Yes.

Officer So, all we need is a job in a forest, by a lake, saving lives. Did you get anything else?

Harry No.

Officer What, did they not give you anything when you left?

Harry I was supposed to hand me P.E. kit in, but I kept it.

Officer And that is the sum total of your academic career?

Harry Yes.

Officer Well, we could put you to an apprenticeship, on the buildings or in a factory.

Harry Apprenticeship is no use. Takes you five years to learn what you could pick up in six months.

Officer You don't want an apprenticeship.

Harry No, but I want Saturday afternoons off.

Officer That leaves you with labouring, or semi-skilled.

Harry I don't want that.

Officer What sort of thing would you like? Now think about it. I can wait. Take your time. I'm patient. I was trained in psychology and all the rest of it. What sort of job would you like?

Harry I would like a job with adventure. Like on the telly. Lots of thrills. Pioneering, life. Colour. Like the pictures. I was brought up on the pictures.

Officer Would you like to try the Police, you've got the height?

Harry I don't like law and order. It usually picks on me. If anything, I would be a cat burglar. But I'm frightened of heights. I keep planning daring daylight robberies but when I get to the stage for shinning up the drainpipe, I can't do it.

Officer Well, all we need to find you is a cat burgling job. Ground floors only. Now come on, come on. I may have done psychology, but I'm not Job. It'll have to be the last stage of a conveyor belt. You can be the human end of a mechanized system, how will that suit you? Like jam. Take jam. The fruit comes in at one end, and is skinned and stoned by a machine, then it is washed and cleaned in a machine, then it is mixed with sugar in a huge boiler, worked by a machine, then it runs off into jars by a machine process. The jars are lidded by a machine; then they are boxed by a machine, then they are all pushed on conveyor belts and pushed along to the loading bay by a machine; and there on the loading bay is you. Lifting them on to a lorry, the human end to a machine system, how would you like that?

Harry Have they got nothing to lift them on with?

Officer The driver likes somebody to talk to. Now, I'll fill you in a pink form, look, it's quite personal. It has your number for filing; and I'll put your name on it though that's not really necessary, but it'll make you feel good. Now, run along, and present that. Say you're from me, Mr Baxter. They know me down there, I've sent them some good lads. And they keep coming back for more. I'd send my own son down there only the lorry driver wouldn't get on with him.

Harry I don't like the idea of a card.

Officer You've got to have a card.

Harry How do I reach the place?

Officer The address is on it, look.
Harry But how do I reach it?
Officer Just step outside son, and ask a policeman. Every man to his job.
(*Exit* **Harry**.)

Youth Careers Officer's Lament

Officer (*sings*)
I've seen better days than this,
I've seen better days than this.
Why in the days of yore
Able-bodied men by the score
Have lined up at my door
Shouting for jobs, shouting for jobs.

I've seen better days before,
I've seen better days before.
Why in between the wars
There'd be stamping on the floors,
And great hungry clamours
Shouting for jobs, shouting for jobs.

I've seen when I had respect,
I've seen when I had respect.
Pitmen, diggers called me sir,
My wife would have fox fur,
And me, a celluloid white collar,
Handing out jobs, handing out jobs.

I've seen better days by far,
I've seen better days by far.
Why outside the walls were polished clean
Where men's shoulders had been
Waiting, strained and lean,
Shouting for jobs, shouting for jobs.

I've seen better days than this,
I've seen better days than this.
Men were once drawers of water, carriers of wood.
Those times for me were good.
I'd have them back again if I could,
Shouting for jobs, shouting for jobs.
(*Exit* **Youth Careers Officer**.)

Chorus (*sing*)

I'm forever blowing bubbles,
Pretty bubbles in the air,
They fly so high,
Nearly reach the sky,
Then like my dreams they fade and die.
Fortune always hiding, I've looked ev'rywhere,
I'm forever blowing bubbles,
Pretty bubbles in the air.

Points for discussion or written work

1. What was your immediate reaction to the technique used here known as 'alienation'? Did the song and chorus help you to understand anything more about the scene—or did the lack of realism spoil the effect?

2. How did the Youth Careers Officer treat Harry? Did he deal with Harry's job enquiry satisfactorily? What improvements could you suggest to make the interview better?

3. Would you agree with Harry's view that apprenticeships take you 'five years to learn what you could pick up in six months', or do you think apprenticeships might have other, longer term benefits? Argue for or against.

4. The Youth Careers Officer's song suggests that in the past people were grateful if he found them work, but that nowadays attitudes to employment and unemployment have changed. Do you agree? Say why.

5. Harry wants 'a job with adventure. Like on the telly Lots of thrills. Pioneering, life, colour. Like the pictures.' Is this a realistic set of requirements? What are your job requirements? Make a list of all the things you consider important. See how they compare with your friends.

6. The chorus at the end is a sad comment on how, quite often, our dreams, hopes and aspirations can come to nothing—'like my dreams they fade and die'. Is this true? Do young people leaving school to-day really face such a bleak future? Try to think of some hopeful points to counter this argument.

7. Imagine you have left school and have applied for a job. Decide what the job is, and invent the name and address of your future employer. He/she has written to your present Headteacher for a reference. Write the letter you think your Headteacher might send in reply.

Suggestions for script or improvisation

1. Script or improvise—you could try the alienation technique—Harry's visit to and interview at, the jam factory. Include a similar large cast because during the scene Harry can be shown the conveyor belt and factory with work in progress. Does he get offered the job, and if so, does he accept? Include a song to be sung by Harry in which he decides whether or not the job measures up to his requirements. Try to end the scene with a chorus when the factory workers join in.

Moving on from there . . .

2. Script or improvise *any* job interview, trying to make it as realistic as possible.

3. 'No Work'. Use this title as the starting point for a script or improvisation. You might investigate here the effect on an individual—or a family—of long-term unemployment.

4. 'Social Security Claimant'. Script an interview between an unemployed labourer and a Social Security Officer. The labourer cannot find work and badly needs money to pay for rent and food for his family: a wife and two young children. You can decide how sympathetic the Social Security Officer is; but make the scene convincing, including as many realistic details as possible.

Arnold Wesker

The Kitchen

The playwright Arnold Wesker was born in Stepney, London, in 1932 He left school at sixteen to work, unsuccessfully, in a variety of jobs from apprentice furniture maker, to carpenter, to bookshop assistant, before eventually doing his National Service in the R.A.F. Later he worked for a time as a pastry-cook in Paris, and perhap this experience provided him with inspiration and material for *The Kitchen*, which he wrote in 1956. Wesker is known for writing plays with a Socialist outlook championing the cause of the working man. Other plays written by him include: *Roots, I'm Talking about Jerusalem*, and *Chips with Everything*.

The play 'The world might have been a stage for Shakespeare', wrote Wesker in an introduction to *The Kitchen*, 'but t me it is a kitchen, where people come and go and cannot stay long enough to understand each other.' Wesker's play is a detailed and realistic study of a busy restaurant kitchen, full of bustle and activity, but it als has much to say about the lives of the people who work there, and indeed about anyone who works for their living. *The Kitchen* was first performed as a one-act play in 1959 and revived in a full-length version in 1961.

The extract The workers in the kitchen are resting after spending a particularly busy morning preparing and serving lunch It is afternoon break. Two characters, Paul and Raymond, are the only ones who are still working in one corner. The others are sitting around, while Dimitri sweeps up.

Characters: how it might be acted **Kevin:** *young Irishman, aged 22. This is his first day in the kitchen. He is disturbed by the mad rush of the work and the people around him.*

Paul/Raymond: *two pastry cooks—calmer than the others. Paul is a young Jew; Raymond an Italian who speaks perfect English, but with an accent.*

Dimitri: *kitchen porter, possibly from Cyprus.*
Peter: *the main character of the play; a young German aged 23; has worked in the kitchen for three years; his parents were killed in the war; he is boisterous, aggressive, and yet at the same time good-natured. After three years of work at this restaurant, he must be living on his nerves.*
Hans: *another young German; sensitive 19 years-old; speaks very bad English and is impressed by anything flashy.*

Setting: the kitchen of the Tivoli Restaurant. Blocks or tables could be arranged to represent cookers, stoves and serving points with a few chairs and a wooden bench on which Kevin is lying flat out. Obviously foreign accents present a major challenge here. If necessary seek advice from Modern Language teachers in your school, but try to develop a sense of accent if possible, although the extract should still work without it.

The Kitchen

Kevin Finished! I'm done! I'm boiled! You can serve me up for supper!

Paul (*as if ordering a meal*) Two portions of boiled Irishman please! With garnish!

Ray. (*also calling*) Two fried tomatoes on his ears, potatoes round his head, and stuff his mouth with an extra helping of peas.

Kevin I'll produce me own gravy! But did you see it? Did-you-see-that? Fifteen hundred customers, an' half of them eating fish. *I* had to start work on a Friday!

Ray. It's every day the same, my friend.

Kevin (*raising himself up*) Look at me. I'm soaking. Look at this jacket. I can wring it out. That's not sweat, no man carries that much water. (*Flopping back again.*) Kevin, you'll drop dead if you stay. I'm warning you Kevin, take a tip from a friend, hop it! Get out! You've got your youth Kevin, keep it! This is no place for a human being—you'll drop dead, I'm telling you.

Dimitri Hey Irishman, what you grumbling about this place for? Is different anywhere else? People come and people go, big excitement, big noise. (*Makes noise and gesticulates.*) What for? In the end who do you know? You make a friend, you going to be all you life his friend but when you go from here—pshtt! You forget! Why you grumble about this one kitchen?

Peter You're a very intelligent boy, Dimitri.

Dimitri And you're a bloody fool. I'm not sure I want to talk with you.

Kevin Oh not the Gaston row again. All the morning I hear how Peter give Gaston a black eye. It's the break, no rows please, it's peace. Can you hear it? It's lovely, it's silence. It's nothing—ahhh! (*Moves.*) Oooh—I'm drowning, in my own sweat. Christ! What a way to die.

Dimitri (*to* **Peter**) A bloody fool you!

(**Peter** *picks up a cardboard box, and puts it over* **Dimitri's** *head.* **Dimitri** *flings it off angrily and is about to throw it back, but he sees* **Peter** *with his head in his hands. Instead, he takes out a cigarette box, and begins rolling* **Peter** *a cigarette. He gives the paper to* **Peter** *to lick, then continues folding it, and hands it to him.*)

Peter Hey Irishman, I thought you didn't like this place. Why don't you go home and sleep?

Kevin Me home is a room and a bed and a painting of the Holy Virgin. It'll always be there.

Peter Like this place, this house—this too, it'll always be here. That's a thought for you Irishman. This—this madhouse it's always here. When you go, when I go, when Dimitri go—this kitchen stays. It'll go on when we die, think about that. We work here—eight hours a day, and yet—it's nothing. We take nothing. Here—the kitchen, here—you. You and the kitchen. And the kitchen don't mean nothing to you and you don't mean to the kitchen nothing. Dimitri is right you know—why do you grumble about this kitchen? What about the offices and the factories? There Irishman—what do you say to that?

Kevin You want to come in one morning and find it gone?

Peter Just one morning. Imagine it, eh? Gone. All this gone.

Kevin So you'd be out of work!

Peter So I'd die?

Kevin It doesn't worry you I suppose.

Hans Du träumst schon wieder.
Kevin What's he say?
Peter He say—I'm dreaming . . .

. . . .

When a man dreams—he grows, big, better. You find that silly?

. . . .

I want to dream. Everyone should dream, once in a life everyone should dream. Hey Irishman, you dream, how do you dream, tell us?
Kevin You play our own games, Peter, leave me out of it, I'm past it.
Peter You know when a man is not a man? When he's ashamed of being a child. That's you Irishman. You're ashamed of being a child. Why you ashamed? We all friends here, why you ashamed to dream, I give you the chance.
Kevin I'm obliged!
Peter Hey Paul, Raymondo, Dimitri, stop work a minute. You got time. Here, come here. We are all given a chance to dream. No one is going to laugh, we love each other, we protect each other—someone tell us a dream, just to us, no one else, the ovens are low, the customers gone, Marango is gone, it's all quiet. God has given us a chance now, we never had the opportunity again, so dream—someone—who? Dimitri—you, you dream first.
Dimitri In this place? With iron around me? And dustbins? And black walls?
Peter Pretend! There's no dustbins. Pretend! The walls are skies, yes? The iron, it's rock on a coast; the tables, (*thinks*) they're rose bushes; and the ovens are the noise of the winds. Look at the lights—stars, Dimitri . . . Dimitri—dream—a little dream, what you see?
Dimitri A little, a little er—what you call it—a small house, sort of—
Paul A hut?
Dimitri No—
Kevin A shed?
Dimitri That's right, a shed. With instruments, and tools, and I make lots of radios and television sets maybe, and . . .
Peter Ach no, silly boy. That's a hobby, that's not what you really want. You want more, more, Dimitri—
Dimitri I—I—I can't, Peter, I can't see more, I try but I can't see more.

Peter Poor Dimitri—hey Irishman, you—you dream.

Kevin If you think because I'm Irish I'm going to start prattling on about goblins and leprechauns you've got another think coming—

Peter No, no, not fairies, a real dream, about men—

Kevin But I don't dream of men—

Peter What then?

Kevin Sleep! Sleep me. Most people sleep and dream; me—I dream of sleep!

Peter What is it with you all? Hans—you, what are your dreams? (**Hans** *sings, as though not answering the question. Then*—)

Hans Money! Geld, Peter, Geld! With money I'm a good man! I'm generous! I love all the world! Money, Pete! Money! Money! Money! (*Continues singing.*)

Peter How can you talk of money, Hans, when you're singing?

Hans Dreaming, mein Lieber, dreaming, dreaming.

Peter Raymondo?

Ray. Me? Women!

Peter Which women? Large, small? Happy? Black? Yellow? What kind?

Ray. There *is* more than one kind?

Peter Raymond—you make me very sad. Paul—you.

Paul Do me a favour.

Peter Please!

Paul No. (*Relents.*) Listen, Peter . . . I'll tell you something. I'm going to be honest with you. You don't mind if I'm honest? Right! I'm going to be honest with you. I don't like you. Now wait a minute, let me finish. I don't like you! I think you're a pig! You bully, you're jealous, you go mad with your work, you always quarrel. All right! But now it's quiet, the ovens are low, the work has stopped for a little and now I'm getting to know you. I still think you're a pig—only now, not so much of a pig. So that's what I dream. I dream of a friend. You give me a rest, you give me silence, you take away this mad kitchen so I make friends, so I think—maybe all the people I thought were pigs are not so much pigs.

Peter You think people are pigs, eh?

Paul Listen, I'll tell you something. I agree with Dimitri also; when the world is filled with kitchens you get pigs—I'll tell you. Next door to me, next door where I live is a bus driver. Comes from Hoxton, he's my age, married and got two kids. He says good-morning to me, I ask him how he is, I give his children sweets.

That's our relationship. Somehow he seems frightened to say too much, you know? God forbid I might ask him for something. So we make no demands on each other. Then one day the busmen go on strike. He's out for five weeks. Every morning I say to him 'Keep going mate, you'll win.' Every morning I give him words of encouragement; I say I understand his cause. I've got to get up earlier to get to work but I don't mind. We're neighbours. We're workers together, he's pleased. (*Pause.*) Then, one Sunday, there's a peace march. I don't believe they do much good but I go, because in this world a man's got to show he can have his say. The next morning he comes up to me and he says, now listen to this, he says 'Did you go on that peace march yesterday?' So I says Yes, I did go on that peace march yesterday. So then he turns round to me and he says, 'You know what? A bomb should have been dropped on the lot of them! It's a pity,' he says, 'that they had children with them cos a bomb should've been dropped on the lot!' And you know what was upsetting him? The march was holding up the traffic, the buses couldn't move so fast! Now I don't want him to say I'm right, I don't want him to agree with what I did, but what terrifies me is that he didn't stop to think that this man helped me in my cause so maybe, only *maybe*, there's something in his cause. I'll talk about it. No! The buses were held up so drop a bomb he says, on the lot! And you should've seen the hate in his eyes, as if I'd murdered his child. Like an animal he looked. And the horror is this—that there's a wall, a big wall between me and millions of people like him. And I think—where will it end? What do you do about it? And I look around me, at the kitchen, at the factories, at the enormous bloody buildings going up with all those offices and all those people in them, and I think, Christ! I think, Christ, Christ, Christ! I agree with you Peter—maybe one morning we should wake up and find them all gone. But then I think: I should stop making pastries? The factory worker should stop making trains and cars? The miner should leave the coals where it is? (*Pause.*) *You* give *me* an answer. You give me your dream.

Kevin Hush pâtissier! Hush! It's quiet now. Gently now. (*There is a long silence. The ovens hum.*)

Peter I ask for dreams—you give me nightmares.

Paul So I've dreamt! Is it my fault if it's a nightmare?

Kevin We're waiting for your dream now, Peter boy.

Dimitri (*jumping up suddenly*) This is the United Nations, eh? A big conference. Is Russia here, and America and France and England—and Germany too. Is all here. And they got on a competition. Is finished the wars, is finished the rows. Everybody gone home. We got time on our hands. A prize of one million dollars for the best dream. Raymondo he want a new woman every night. I want a workshop. Paul he wants a friend. Irishman he wants a bed and Hans he just want the million dollars. Big opportunity! Come on Peter, a big dream.

Peter (*looking around*) All this gone?

Dimitri You said so. One morning you come here, to this street here, and the kitchen is gone. And you look around for more kitchens and is none anywhere. What you want to do? The United Nations wants to know.

Paul Come on, come on!

Peter Shush, shush!

(**Peter** *suddenly confronted with his own idea becomes embarrassed and shy. He laughs.*)

Peter I can't. I can't. . . .

Points for discussion or written work

1. When Peter says, 'the kitchen don't mean nothing to you and you don't mean to the kitchen nothing,' what do you think he means? Do you agree, or is it possible to find personal satisfaction in your working occupation? Try to think of some examples of job satisfaction, and what might be valuable qualities in an employee.

2. In trying to get people to tell him their 'dreams', Peter does not seem to get very far. Why might this be? Was it just their shyness, or could it be that working in such a place might stifle personal hopes and aspirations?

3. What serious point does Paul's long speech about his neighbour, the bus driver, make about human tolerance? Say what you think he means by the term the 'big wall'.

4. Do you sympathise with what Paul seems to be saying when he refers to the 'kitchens . . . factories . . . and all those offices'. Is life in such places intolerable? Can you think of some positive features of working in, say, a large factory? What are the disadvantages?

5. Why, in the end couldn't Peter tell the others his 'dreams'?

6. Imagine you are looking for a job in a kitchen. Write a properly set-out letter to The Proprietor, The Tivoli Restaurant, Greek Street, London SW1A 2PP, outlining your age and qualifications, and stating what job you seek. Make the letter as convincing and detailed as possible. You can invent suitable qualifications.

7. Write a complete set of menus for a day at the Tivoli Restaurant. Start with a three-course breakfast, and include a three-course lunch, followed by a four-course dinner. Include several choices for each course; research accurate prices.

Suggestions for script or improvisation

1. Improvise or script a busy kitchen scene, working at full pitch. Include several chefs, and waiters/waitresses shouting orders as they come in from an imaginary dining room. Try to make the ordinary working of the kitchen as realistic and busy as possible. Then, one of the waiters returns with a portion which for some reason (this is up to you) has been sent back by a customer. Chefs are not always very patient . . . an argument develops . . . other waiters and chefs can get involved . . . How is it all resolved?

Moving on from there . . .

2. Improvise or script a scene with the title 'First Day at Work', where a newcomer starts work at either a large factory or an office.

3. Set up an improvisation in a busy factory workshop where a group of workers—say five or six—are employed. One of them is lazy and does as little work as possible—how do the others get on with him? Try to get round to dealing with his laziness at some point in the improvisation, but build up a realistic work situation first. You can include a Works Foreman or Manager if you wish.

4. Use the following titles as starters for script or improvisation: 'A Job with Prospects'; 'You're Fired!'; 'Nine to Five Boredom'.

Keith Waterhouse and Willis Hall

Marital Union

The playwrights Biographical details about Waterhouse and Hall can be found under 'A Many Splendoured Thing'.

The play 'Marital Union' is another sketch from the revue *England Our England*, details of which may also be found under 'A Many Splendoured Thing'.

The extract 'Marital Union' is a clever piece of dialogue which on one level is about marriage, being a conversation between husband and wife. However, it is also a witty comment on our use of language, and the way in which 'jargon' is increasingly affecting our everyday lives, particularly when trades union negotiations are being reported in newspapers, and on radio and television.

Characters: how it might be acted **Sidney/Edna:** *no specific age has been given for either character. The only requirement is that both should be working-class. How might this be indicated?*

The authors, in a production note, suggest that at the beginning of the sketch the speech should be realistic and natural, but that it should become more 'stylized' as the characters relapse more and more into their trade-union jargon. On stage the sketch was performed quite simply using only a table and two chairs.

Marital Union

(*A working-class home. The telephone rings and* **Mrs Edna Newbould**, *who has been getting the dinner ready, crosses to answer it.*)

Edna Hullo? No, this is Mrs Newbould speaking. Edna Newbould. No, that's Mr Newbould you want. My husband. No, I'm joint area secretary of the Amalgamated Punch Operators and Associated Trades Unions. It's my husband who is convener of the Sheet Metal Workers Union. Only he's out at the moment. Only I don't think he'd have any statement to make, on that issue. No, well, you see, it is subject to ratification by his committee, so he wouldn't be in any position to make a statement. Thank you. Good-bye.

(*Over the above* **Sidney Newbould** *has entered in his working clothes. He hangs up his coat, takes off his bicycle clips, crosses and kisses* **Edna** *on the cheek.*)

Sidney Who was that, then?

Edna Only the Press. About your Minimum Hours Agreement.

Sidney I hope you told them no com-ment.

Edna I did, I told them no statement.

(**Sidney** *sits and begins going through official-looking envelopes on the table while* **Edna** *bustles about laying the table.*)

How did it go, then?

Sidney I've had a hell of a day. I had a works committee meeting this morning, represented No. 4 workshop at joint consultations committee this afternoon, and I was just coming home and blow me if I didn't have to convene the canteen representatives.

Edna I've only been home ten minutes. Because I had to take Eileen Fairclough's case up at district level. Anyway, we've got her that compensation.

Sidney Did the coalman come, then?

Edna Yes. He left two bags.

Sidney What about the bedroom window, then? You won't have had a chance to do anything about that?

Edna Oh, I raised the matter. I made representations.

Sidney On what level?

Edna At rentman level.

Sidney Oh, it's no use raising it at rentman level, love. He hasn't got the authorization. You want to raise it at landlord level.

Edna I raised it at landlord level last week. I've had extensive negotiations with the landlord. Only it's inconclusive. He keeps on referring it back for further discussion.

Sidney Well, that's no use. It's been broken two weeks, that sashcord.

Edna You don't have to tell me, Sidney. It's me that has it to struggle with.

Sidney Well, we want satisfaction. Did you make personal representation or did you just ring him up?

Edna I rung him up. I was on that phone for half an hour.

Sidney It's no use ringing him up. Go down and see him.

Edna You go down and see him!

Sidney Damn it all, lass, I've delegated you mandatory powers to bring the matter to a satisfactory conclusion. It's no use trying to refer it to husband level at this stage.

Edna (*bitterly*) No, that's the trouble with this house. Everything's got to be done at wife level.

Sidney Well, that's what you're here for.

Edna I'm not here to do all the work. Not to wait on you hand and foot. We had a clear agreement, we were going to share the work. And what did you do? You repudiated it.

Sidney It wasn't me who repudiated it, Edna, it was you. You broke faith. Take the washing up. Perfectly simple—you were going to do the washing, I was going to do the drying. What did you do? You started a protracted demarcation dispute.

Edna You know very well what happened there. I went round to my mother's. I took it to arbitration.

Sidney Arbitration? Arbitration? She couldn't arbitrate the back of our house without showing flagrant prejudice. There was no need to take it to arbitration. We could have sat down round the table and thrashed out our differences. God damn it all, they were only of an internal nature.

Edna It's all right you saying. It's me that has all the work to do. I get no opportunity for recreational activity at all.

Sidney I take the greatest exception to that statement, Edna. I took you to the pictures only last week. At Odeon level.

Edna It's more than a question of going out, Sidney. We've got no cohesion as a family unit, that's our trouble.

Sidney I suppose that's my fault.

Edna Well, whose fault is it?

Sidney It's not mine. (*Brooding for a moment.*) How long is it since you co-operated with me?

Edna On what basis?

Sidney You know what basis.

Edna (*beginning to sob*) That's not the final solution to our deadlock,

Sidney. The unrest goes deeper than that.

Sidney (*kindly*) Now then, come on love, there's no call for a spontaneous demonstration.

(*She allows him to comfort her.*)

Edna (*wiping her eyes*) Well—

Sidney (*gently*) We can discuss matters amicably on an informal level, love. There's no necessity for a split between us. We must sink our differences in the common interest.

Edna Oh, Sidney, I keep thinking our negotiations have broken down.

Sidney No, no, love, there's a very strong bond between us. After all, we are married, aren't we?

Edna Yes, Sidney.

Sidney Well—marriage is a union.

(**Edna**'*s face lights up—they embrace.*)

Blackout

Topics for discussion or written work

1. We find this sketch very amusing—but can you try to say *why* it is funny?

2. Think of some recent examples of trades union negotiations which you have either read about in newspapers, or heard on radio or television. Was similar language used? Make a list of some of the terms which were used.

3. What do the following words or phrases used in the sketch mean? Look them up in a dictionary if you do not know.
1) convener 2) ratification 3) representations
4) delegated 5) mandatory powers 6) repudiated
7) protracted demarcation dispute 8) arbitration
9) flagrant prejudice 10) recreational activity
11) cohesion 12) deadlock.

4. Do some research about the growth and development of trades unions, and write a short history of the movement based on your notes. Find out what trades unions do for their members today, other than argue about pay rises. Will you join a union when you go to work? Why?

5. Find out what the term 'closed shop' means with regard to unions. Is this a good idea?

6. Some people believe that certain categories of workers should never go on strike. Make a list of all those you can think of. Do you agree? Say why. If they shouldn't go on strike, how could their interests be protected?

7. A group of nurses in *Quiet Glades*, an old people's home, have walked out on strike for higher pay, leaving only two nurses to look after 40 residents. Write a well-argued and properly set-out letter to the local newspaper, *The Weekly Herald*, condemning or defending their decision (depending on your personal opinion). Remember to invent full names and addresses both for yourself and the Editor of the newspaper.

Suggestions for script or improvisation

1. Script an interview between a trades union 'convener' and the industrial relations manager of a large factory, using some of the terms mentioned in 'Marital Union' and any others you have heard or read recently. Decide very carefully the nature of the problem they will discuss, and the reactions each will have during their negotiation.

Moving on from there . . .

2. Improvise or script a scene with the title 'Union Dispute', set either on the shop floor of a large Midlands car factory or in the typing pool of a large insurance company.

3. Improvise a scene in a large, busy office. One of the girls in the typing pool is accused of stealing. A union official has to accompany her to the Manager's office and represent her in the interview that follows. Include as many characters as you wish.

4. Eileen, the tea-lady, has worked at Robinson's for almost forty years. She is just sixty next week and the company wants her to retire (so that they can install a vending machine to save costs). Eileen still feels fit and healthy, and wants to continue working, as she realises she would be lonely without the company of her workmates. Improvise or script a scene where Eileen tells her friends at Robinson's that the management is trying to force her to retire against her will. You can decide what happens. Do they accept Eileen's fate and organise a farewell party; does the union intervene; or do the workers act themselves?

The Space between People

From the earliest days of our childhood, the process of 'getting on' with others, of forming friendships and developing the ability to work with, talk and listen to other people, is an important part of our lives.

These plays and sketches investigate 'the space between people'—the problems and difficulties human beings sometimes find in making meaningful relationships.

The last extract, *City Sugar*, looks at communication in a much wider sense: the mass communication involved in running a commercial radio station.

The pictures are all examples of people communicating in one form or another. Use them as starters for improvisation, script, or story.

Harold Pinter

Last to Go

The playwright

Harold Pinter was born in London in 1930 and is generally regarded as one of the most important and original writers to have emerged from the 'new wave' o British dramatists. This was a group of writers who gave fresh life to the British theatre in the late 1950s and early 1960s by writing plays which were often a direct and stark reflection of contemporary life as they saw it. Many of Pinter's plays, for example, show human beings failing to communicate with each other, and individuals desperately, and largely unsuccessfully struggling to establish their personal identity in a grey and unfriendly world. The plays are all firmly based in everyday reality, but Pinter's characters, in their search for some sort of truth, can only find questions, because in real life, do we ever find definite answers? Harold Pinter's many successful plays include: *The Birthday Party*, *The Caretaker* and *No Man's Land*. He has also directed many plays and written for film and television.

The play

'Last to Go' is a complete sketch from a revue called *Pieces of Eight* which was first performed in London on 23 September 1959.

The extract

This sketch is set at a coffee stall late at night. It is a simple conversation between two men, but underneath this is a deeper comment on human relationships.

Characters: how it might be acted

Man: *an old newspaper seller*
Barman: *age not specified; runs a late night coffee stall, probably on the Embankment in London.*

Try reading this sketch using a Cockney accent for both characters. Think of things for each character to do during the pauses—for instance, the man could stir and sip his tea, the barman make sandwiches or wipe the counter. Do not hurry the dialogue—remember it is late at night when all the crowds have gone home. The real skill is in trying to portray the quiet isolation and self-absorption of each character. In a sense, silence is as important as words in this scene.

Use blocks or an old table raised to make it almost chest height for the barman.

Last To Go

(*A coffee stall. A* **Barman** *and an old* **Newspaper Seller**. *The* **Barman** *leans on his counter, the* **Old Man** *stands with tea. Silence.*)

Man You was a bit busier earlier.

Barman Ah.

Man Round about ten.

Barman Ten, was it?

Man About then.

(*Pause.*)

I passed by here about then.

Barman Oh yes?

Man I noticed you were doing a bit of trade.

(*Pause.*)

Barman Yes, trade was very brisk here about ten.

Man Yes, I noticed.

(*Pause.*)

I sold my last one about then. Yes. About nine forty-five.

Barman Sold your last then, did you?

Man Yes, my last 'Evening News' it was. Went about twenty to ten.

(*Pause.*)

Barman 'Evening News', was it?

Man Yes.

(*Pause.*)

Sometimes it's the 'Star' is the last to go.

Barman Ah.

Man Or the . . . whatsisname.

Barman 'Standard'.

Man Yes.

(*Pause.*)

All I had left tonight was the 'Evening News'.

(*Pause.*)

Barman Then that went, did it?

Man Yes.

(*Pause.*)
Like a shot.
(*Pause.*)

Barman You didn't have any left, eh?

Man No. Not after I sold that one.
(*Pause.*)

Barman It was after that you must have come by here then, was it?

Man Yes, I come by here after that, see, after I packed up.

Barman You didn't stop here though, did you?

Man When?

Barman I mean, you didn't stop here and have a cup of tea then, did you?

Man What, about ten?

Barman Yes.

Man No, I went up to Victoria.

Barman No, I thought I didn't see you.

Man I had to go up to Victoria.
(*Pause.*)

Barman Yes, trade was very brisk here about then.
(*Pause.*)

Man I went to see if I could get hold of George.

Barman Who?

Man George.
(*Pause.*)

Barman George who?

Man George . . . whatsisname.

Barman Oh.
(*Pause.*)
Did you get hold of him?

Man No. No, I couldn't get hold of him. I couldn't locate him.

Barman He's not about much now, is he?
(*Pause.*)

Man When did you last seen him then?

Barman Oh, I haven't seen him for years.

Man No, nor me.
(*Pause.*)

Barman Used to suffer very bad from arthritis.

Man Arthritis?

Barman Yes.

Man He never suffered from arthritis.

Barman Suffered very bad.

(*Pause.*)

Man Not when I knew him.

(*Pause.*)

Barman I think he must have left the area.

(*Pause.*)

Man Yes, it was the 'Evening News' was the last to go tonight.

Barman Not always the last though, is it, though?

Man No. Oh no. I mean sometimes it's the 'News'. Other times it's one of the others. No way of telling beforehand. Until you've got your last one left, of course. Then you can tell which one it's going to be.

Barman Yes.

(*Pause.*)

Man Oh yes.

(*Pause.*)

I think he must have left the area.

Points for discussion or written work

1. What is the most noticeable feature of the conversation between the two men? Do they *really* listen to each other—how can we tell?

2. How do we know that the 'George' mentioned in the sketch is not the same man for each character? Do either of the characters realise they are not talking about the same man?

3. Could this sort of conversation take place in real life? Is it realistic? Think of similar examples you may have overheard—or even taken part in.

4. Imagine you are a director staging this sketch. Write a detailed description of your visualisation of these two characters, having read the sketch several times. Say what each would look like, wear, and how each would talk.

5. Draw a stage plan and a three-dimensional drawing of the set you would use. Make a list of any stage props you would need.

6. Write a story following one or both characters home after the coffee stall has closed.

Suggestions for script or improvisation

1. Improvise or script a similar scene where two characters meet and have a very ordinary conversation without *really* listening to each other. You could set it at a late night coffee stall, like Pinter, or in another setting—two men in a public house, or two old people reminiscing, for example. Imitate Pinter's style as closely as possible, especially the relaxed use he makes of pauses and silence.

Moving on from there . . .

2. Improvise or script another scene with the same title, 'Last to Go', but think of something other than newspapers.

3. Use the title 'Does Anyone Care?' as the starting point for a scripted or improvised scene which investigates the problem of loneliness.

4. Write or improvise a script for two down-and-outs. It is late at night; both are cold, hungry and full of despair. Does anything happen to them; does anyone come along and offer them food, warmth or shelter; or do we leave them at the end of the scene as we found them at the beginning?

N.F. Simpson

One Blast and Have Done

The playwright N.F. Simpson was born in London in 1919. After obtaining a degree at London University, he became a teacher. In 1957, he was awarded third prize in a play competition organised by the *Observer* for *A Resounding Tinkle*. His plays are not realistic, but he has been called 'a more powerful social critic than any of the social realists'. He usually sets his plays in very ordinary suburban settings, in which his somewhat extraordinary characters abandon everyday logic. In another of his plays, *One Way Pendulum*, for example, one of the characters builds up his savings by feeding coins into his own parking meters, while his son vainly attempts to train a collection of 'Speak Your Weight' machines to sing the 'Hallelujah Chorus'! Such drama is known as Theatre of the Absurd.

The play 'One Blast and Have Done' is a complete sketch in its own right, and compliments Pinter's 'Last to Go'. Like Pinter, Simpson creates a familiar enough situation: a surburban housewife popping round to borrow something from her neighbour. However the 'something' she asks for and the conversation which ensues is far from normal; but although what happens is 'absurd', the language which Simpson's characters use remains strikingly familiar. 'One Blast and Have Done' was first published in the *Queen* magazine on 28 September 1960.

Characters: how it might be acted **Freda/Ivy:** *age for both women unspecified. Try experimenting with accent and mannerisms to exploit the humour to the full. Neither character should show any surprise at the absurdities in the dialogue. Great control is needed when acting this to avoid laughing.*

Setting: an ordinary living room or kitchen. Two chairs and a table would suffice, though a teapot and two cups would add extra authenticity.

One Blast and Have Done

Freda Ivy!

Ivy Hello, Freda.

Freda Come in. Sit down and have a cup of tea.

Ivy No, thank you, Freda. I mustn't stop. I'm on the cadge really. You wouldn't have such a thing as a flute? We've had a flautist call.

Freda A flute. Goodness.

Ivy No warning or anything.

Freda I'm just trying to think, Ivy. I know we did have one.

Ivy We haven't got a thing in the house except percussion.

Freda I suppose a bassoon wouldn't do? If I can find one.

Ivy Anything at all, Freda.

Freda I'll see what there is in the cupboard.

Ivy As long as it's something he can blow down.

Freda He wants to be able to blow across it, really, if he's a flautist but . . . no, there's only this. Would that do, do you think? It's one of mum's old bassoons. She never uses it.

Ivy That would do fine, Freda.

Freda I think it works all right. As long as he doesn't mind a bit of coal dust in it.

Ivy If you're sure you can spare it.

Freda Let me put a duster over it for you. Get some of the worst off.

Ivy Don't bother, Freda.

Freda It won't take a minute.

Ivy He could have made do with it as it was.

Freda I wish I knew where to put my hands on a flute for you. There's one somewhere I'm almost certain. We had an old harmonium with a flute in it at one time but I don't know till Tom gets in what he's done with it.

Ivy It doesn't matter, Freda. This is fine.

Freda Tell him to mind the coal dust inside when he starts to blow.

Ivy It gets into everything, doesn't it?

Freda We had *coal* once.

Ivy No!

Freda We did. In the American organ. Great lumps the size of cricket balls.

Ivy How on earth did that happen?

Freda We made the mistake of lending it to some people we knew down the road. And that's how it came back.

Ivy With coal in it.

Freda And all stuck in any old how, of course. At the back and underneath.

Ivy It's not right, is it?

Freda No attempt at putting all the big lumps together, or separating out the slack, or anything like that.

Ivy Too much trouble.

Freda Under the bellows and everywhere. I said to Tom—you'll never play it while it's in that state.

Ivy It's not the place for it.

Freda He had a rousing tune he could have played if it hadn't been for that. Nearly a hundredweight of it altogether there must have been when we cleared it out.

Ivy Fancy.

Freda What's that noise?

Ivy I didn't hear anything.

Freda I thought I heard knocking.
(*Knocks are heard on wall.*)

Ivy You're right. He's getting impatient for his flute.

Freda Who is it? If it's not a rude question.

Ivy I've never set eyes on him before, Freda, in my life. Just came in, out of the blue, about half an hour ago.

Freda You haven't left him in there by himself?

Ivy Yes—I'd better go back. Before he starts getting up to anything. This is the second one we've had this week.

Freda Go on?

Ivy We had one in on Monday. They seem to be making a bee-line for us for some reason.

Freda And what did *he* want?

Ivy Could he come in for a minute and beat hell out of our timpani, if you please!

Freda No!

Ivy No credentials or anything, of course.

Freda Isn't it the limit?

Ivy Tried to tell me he was over here on a day trip from Vladivostock.

Freda *That* speaks volumes.

Ivy Looking for his brother.

Freda Just as well it was a Monday.

Ivy In any case, even if he was genuine, you don't want complete strangers walking in whenever they feel like it and going for all they're worth at your timpani.

Freda Of course you don't. (*Knocking repeated.*) There he is again. He's getting impatient.

Ivy (*shouts*) I'm just coming. (*To* **Freda**.) If it had been anything but timpani I should very likely have fallen for it, but it so happened I was saving the timpani for Fred and Doris when they came in, so they could have a bit of percussion before they went to bed. Otherwise I might have let him in. (*Knocking repeated.*)

Freda You'll have him singing in there, Ivy. All over the furniture.

Ivy (*going*) Goodness—don't say that. I don't want that happening. I've had enough singing to last *me* for a little while. I didn't tell you about Wednesday, did I?

Freda Not Mrs Bargold again?

Ivy (*returning*) You know what a nice afternoon it was, Wednesday—after it brightened up. So I thought I'll just have half an hour with a book out in the garden while I can. . . .

Freda And Mrs Bargold started up.

Ivy Started up! I've never heard anything like it. Right through the trellis-work.

Freda It isn't as if she's exactly a Peach Melba, either.

Ivy I stuck it for as long as I could, but. . . .

Freda She must have a sixth sense.

Ivy Every time I sit down out there. In the end I called over to her. I couldn't stand it any longer. I said I don't mind you singing, Mrs Bargold—but not through my trellis-work if you don't mind.

Freda It's not as if it's just once or twice, is it?

Ivy *Rock of Ages*. Full blast at the top of her voice.

Freda *Rock of Ages?* That's a change, isn't it?

Ivy Right through the trellis-work. I couldn't read or do anything.

Freda I don't think I've heard Mrs Bargold sing *Rock of Ages* since Mr Stepupper called her in to sing down the overflow pipe while the stopcock was being seen to.

Ivy I told her — I didn't have trellis-work put up for her to sing *Rock of Ages* through whenever it happened to suit her convenience.

Freda Of course not.

Ivy It's not cheap, either. Ten-and-six a yard it was, all told, to put up. With the labour.

Freda I can imagine.

. . . .

Ivy And do you know what she had the cheek to say to me? She sai I was the first one who'd complained! (*mimicking*) 'No one else has ever complained.'

Freda Only because they knew it wouldn't make any difference.

Ivy 'No one else has complained!' I said to her—no one else has ha *Rock of Ages* sung through their trellis-work week after week fo months on end.

(*A single, prolonged, loud note from a trombone is heard.*)

What was that?

Freda It sounded like a trombone, Ivy.

Ivy (*going off*) What's he getting up to in there?

Freda (*loudly, after her*) He couldn't wait, I expect. He's blown down the nearest thing.

(*Pause. Then in an undertone, sardonically.*)

'Nothing in the house except percussion!'

Curtain

Points for discussion or written work

1. How does Simpson succeed in making such an exaggerated and obviously unrealistic sketch so amusing? What do we laugh *at* in this sketch?

2. Pick out all the phrases in the conversation between Ivy and Freda which we can recognise as being both normal and what we might hear being spoken by suburban housewives. How are they then made *absurd*?

3. Does Simpson have anything serious to say about these two women—or neighbours in general—or is this sketch meant simply to be for pure amusement and enjoyment?

4. What do you think Ivy and Freda look like? How would they dress? Write a full description of each character.

Suggestions for script or improvisation

1. Improvise or script a scene where two neighbours meet to gossip. You might use two people hanging out their washing, or cleaning their cars. You could try imitating Simpson's Absurd style.

Moving on from there . . .

2. Improvise or script a scene where two sets of neighbours eventually have a disagreement. One family are spending a quiet Sunday afternoon sunbathing and having tea in their garden, when their neighbours come out—complete with transistor radio, to work, rather noisily, on their car. . . .

3. 'Did you hear about that woman down the road?' Use this as the opening line of a script or improvisation for two characters.

Mike Leigh

Abigail's Party

The playwright Mike Leigh, born in 1943, was trained as an actor at The Royal Academy of Dramatic Arts. His first job was as Assistant Stage Manager at a repertory company in Leatherhead. From there he went on in 1967 to work with Peter Hall as an assistant director at The Royal Shakespeare Theatre, Stratford-upon-Avon. After this he left to teach in an acting school, and then spent a year training to be a teacher before returning to work in the theatre and in film. His many successful television plays include *Grown-ups* and *Nuts in May*.

The play *Abigail's Party* is unusual in that it appears not to have actually been written! Instead it was 'devised' by Mike Leigh after a series of improvisations with the actors who later took parts in the play. Each actor discussed with Leigh their own character, and between them they created a complete identity. Leigh then developed these characters from the improvisations, polishing these situations into the more conventional dramatic form of a script. *Abigail's Party* portrays an evening when two parties are being held. The audience never actually witnesses Abigail's party, as this is being given in a neighbouring house, but on stage, Beverly and Laurence have drinks with Angela and Tony, a couple who live nearby, and Susan, Abigail's divorced mother. As the evening progresses, the conversation develops from superficial and almost meaningless small-talk to a point where the characters begin to reveal something of their real personalities and problems.

The extract Laurence and Beverly are expecting guests for drinks. If the play is being staged the general effect of their living room should be bright, brash, 'modern and labour-saving'. Some might say tasteless. If not, several chairs and a coffee table would suffice.

Characters: how it might be acted

Beverly: *late thirties; heavily made-up and probably over-dressed; dominant and quite aggressive; has an affected, almost whining accent; is attracted to Tony.*
Laurence: *Beverly's husband: a busy 'scurrying' estate agent, about the same age as his wife.*
Angela: *younger than Beverly; very plain; a nurse who never thought anyone would marry her.*
Tony: *Angela's husband; late twenties; very athletic; quite good-looking; 'strong but silent' type; possibly wonders if he has done the right thing marrying his talkative wife.*
Susan: *early middle-aged; quiet and more refined than the others.*

Try exaggerated accents for Beverly and Angela accentuating the fact that they are rather 'common', though of course neither realise it. Beverly even considers that she has 'taste'.

Abigail's Party

(*The ground floor of Laurence and Beverly's house. An early evening in Spring.* **Laurence** *and* **Beverly** *are sitting with drinks, just before their guests arrive.*
The front doorbell chimes.)

Laur. (*jumping up*) They're early, aren't they?
Beverly No they're not. And you've not changed.
Laur. I know that. (*He goes to answer the door.*)
(**Laurence** *exits.*
Beverly *composes herself, then rises, and prepares to receive guests, going to the door.*)
Angela (*off*) Hello, you must be Laurence!
Laur. (*off*) That's right.
Angela (*off*) I'm Angie.
Laur. (*off*) Do go in, won't you?
Angela (*off*) Thank you. This is my husband, Tony.
Tony (*off*) How d'you do.
Laur. (*off*) Hullo.
(**Angela**, **Laurence** *and* **Tony** *come in.*)
Beverly Hi, Ang.
Angela Hello, Beverly—what a lovely dress!

Beverly Thanks.
Angela Were we meant to wear long?
Beverly No, no, it's just informal, you know . . .
Angela This is my husband, Tony.
Beverly How d'you do, pleased to meet you.
Tony How d'you do.
Beverly He's got a firm handshake, hasn't he?
Angela Yes.
Beverly Yeah, fantastic. Like to go through?
Tony Ta.
Angela This is the suite I was telling you about. It's nice, isn't it?
Tony Lovely.
Angela We've just bought a new three-piece suite, but ours isn't real leather, like this—it's 'leather look'.
Beverly Oh, the Leather Look? Great.
Laur. Drink?
Tony Yes, please.
Beverly Laurence, would you like to take Angela's coat, please?
Laur. Surely.
Angela Thanks.
Laur. Pleasure
(**Laurence** *takes* **Angela**'*s coat out*.)
Beverly It's funny, 'cos he's a lot bigger than I thought he was. Yeah—'cos I've seen him across the road, Ang, and I thought he was about the same size as Laurence—
Angela Oh, no . . .
Beverly —but he's not, he's a lot bigger, yeah, great. Would you like a drink?
Tony Yes, please.
Beverly What would you like?
Tony Bacardi and Coke, please.
Beverly Ice and Lemon?
Tony Yes, please.
Beverly Great. How about you, Ang?
Angela Have you got gin?
Beverly Gin and tonic?
Angela Please.
Beverly Ice and lemon?
Angela Yes, please.
Beverly Great.
(**Laurence** *enters*)
Laurence, would you like to get the drinks, please? Tony would

like Bacardi and Coke with ice and lemon, Angela would like gin and tonic with ice and lemon, and I'd like a little fill-up, okay?

Laur. Surely.

Beverly D'you like lager, Tony?

Tony I'll be all right with Bacardi, thank you.

Beverly No—as a chaser, a little bit later on; because Laurence is gonna get some.

Tony It'll be okay, thank you.

Beverly Or a light ale. Which d'you prefer?

Tony Light ale.

Beverly Light ale? Laurence, would you get some light ale as well, please?

Laur. Yes.

Beverly Actually, Ang, it's going to be really nice, because I've invited Sue from Number Nine.

Angela Oh, lovely.

Beverly Yeah, so I thought it'd be nice for you to meet her as well. Yeah, 'cos her daughter's having a party. Well, she's only a teenager, so I said, well pop down and spend the evening with us.

Angela That'd be really nice, 'cos I want to meet all the neighbours.

Beverly Yeah, just say hello, Ang, and break the ice.

Angela 'Cos that was what was so nice when you came over, 'cos it really made me feel at home.

Beverly Well, Ang, I know what I felt like when I moved in—I was lonely. So I thought, well, that's not going to happen to you.

Angela Well, you're the friendly type, aren't you?

Beverly Yeah, yeah. It's funny, 'cos as soon as we met, I knew we were gonna get on.

Angela Well, we're alike, aren't we?

Beverly Yeah, yeah.
(**Laurence** *gives* **Angela** *and* **Beverly** *their drinks.*)
Thanks.

Angela Thanks.
(**Laurence** *gives* **Tony** *his drink.*)

Tony Thank you.

Beverly Cheers, everyone!

Angela Cheers!

Beverly Cheers, Tone!

Tony Cheers.
(**Laurence** *gets his glass from the coffee table.*)

Laur. Cheers!

Angela Cheers!

Beverly What are you doing, darling? Are you staying, or going?

Laur. Er, I'll stay for a while.

Beverly Laurence has to pop out on business, I'm afraid, so . . . Now: anybody like a cigarette? Laurence, would you, please? (**Laurence** *offers the cigarette box.*) Angela?

Angela No, thanks.

Beverly Tony, would you like a cigarette?

Tony No, thank you.

Angela We've just given up.

Beverly Oh, yeah. Sorry!

Laur. Now, who'd like some olives?

Beverly Not for me. Ang?

Angela No, thanks.

Beverly Tony, d'you like olives?

Tony No, I don't.

Beverly No, they're horrible, aren't they?

Angela Yes.

Beverly They've got a very bitter taste, haven't they, Ang?

Angela Yes.

Beverly I told you nobody'd like olives, Laurence.

Laur. Not nobody, Beverly: I like olives. And that's twenty-five per cent of the assembled company.

Angela We've met you before, haven't we?

Laur. Really?

Angela He is the one you remember, isn't he?

Tony Yeah.

Angela D'you remember us? We came looking for a house.

Laur. I can't say I do; of course we see a lot of clients.

Tony We saw a lot of estate agents.

Angela Yes, we went to all the ones in the area. We got the house from Spencer's in the end—Anthony Spencer.

Beverly Oh, Anthony Spencer, yeah, yeah.

Angela Well it was Nicholas Spencer who was dealing with us.

Beverly Yeah?

Angela He's very nice. D'you know him?

Laur. Yes, I know him.

Angela Have you seen those boards they have outside?

Beverly Ang, aren't they beautiful?

Angela Yes, they're lovely. With the house and the family and the car and the tree. When I saw them I thought, 'I hope we get a house with one of those boards.' I expect they sell a lot of houses because of the boards. Don't you think so?

Laur. No actually, I don't.

Angela Oh, don't you? We were very lucky, actually, 'cos we got the price of the house down from twenty-two thousand to twenty-one thousand.

Beverly Really? Oh that is fantastic, Ang, that's really great.

(*During the following,* **Beverly** *offers cheese-pineapple savouries to* **Angela** *and* **Tony**. *So does* **Laurence**, *though superfluously as it turns out.* **Tony** *says 'ta' where appropriate.*)

Is it your first house?

Angela Yes, we were in a furnished flat before.

Beverly Oh, that's a bit grim, isn't it, furnished flat? Yeah.

Angela Yes. Well it was nice for us while we were saving.

Beverly Yeah.

Angela But the trouble is, with it being furnished, it means we haven't got much furniture of our own together yet.

Beverly Yeah, and you feel it when you move, don't you?

Angela Yes.

Beverly (*sitting*) Mind you, Ang, your house is smaller than this one, yeah, because I know they are are smaller on your side, yeah.

Angela Yes. Mmm. These are lovely.

Beverly Yes, they're dainty, aren't they?

(*Pause.*)

Laur. What line of business are you in?

Tony } (*speaking together*) Computers.
Angela } He's in computers.

Beverly Oh, really, Tone? That's funny, 'cos my brother's in computers, actually.

Angela Is he?

Beverly Yeah, he's a—programmes analyst.

Angela Oh yes? Tony's just an operator.

Beverly I know it's a fantastic job, though, Tone, 'cos my brother, he had to go to college and get exams. I mean, he was studying for years, wasn't he Laurence?

Laur. Oh, yes.

Beverly Did you have to do all that, Tone—go to college?

Angela You didn't really, did you?

Tony No.

Angela No.

Beverly I know it is a fantastic job, though, Tone, 'cos my brother, he's got a fabulous house and he gets great wages, y'know? Yeah.

Laur. Nine to five is it?

Tony No, it's not, actually; there's quite a bit of variation.

Angela Shift-work.

Tony It's a two-weekly system: one week I work from eight in the morning till four in the afternoon, and the following week I work from four till midnight. I get every other Saturday off.

Beverly Oh, great. Were you off today, Tone?

Tony Yeah, I was, actually.

Angela Yes. It's lucky, 'cos if I'm working on a Saturday, he can do all the shopping.

Beverly Don't you find shopping boring, though, Ang?

Angela Mmm.

Beverly Oh, I do—I hate it. He takes me down in the car, and I get me wheely, Tone, and I whizz in, and I grab anything I can see, and I bung it in the wheely, he writes me a cheque, we bung it in the car, bring it home, and it's done for the week, d'you know what I mean?

Laur. Beverly is not very organized: she doesn't believe in making shopping-lists. You have a car, do you?

Tony Yeah.

Angela Yes, an Escort.

Laur. A yellow one?

Angela That's it.

Laur. Yes, I've seen it.

Beverly Yeah, it's beautiful, actually.

Angela Beverly was saying you only like Minis.

Laur. No, not at all. I don't only like Minis—I like lots of other cars. But I find the Mini economical, efficient and reliable, and the most suited to my purposes. Of course, I change my car every year.

Beverly Yeah, but what I say, Ang, is this: what is the point in changing your car if all you change is the colour?

Laur. That's not all you change, Beverly; the design does alter. But then you're not a motorist, so of course you just don't understand these things.

Beverly Yeah, okay. I know I failed my test three times.

Laur. Three times.

Beverly But, I'm his wife, Ang, and I reckon a wife should have a little say in the choosing of a car.

Laur. Well, when you've passed your test, Beverly, then you can have your little say. Until then, please leave it to me.

Beverly Let me put it to you this way, Ang. When we chose the furniture, we chose it together; when we chose the house, we chose it together; but, when it comes to the car, I'm not allowed to have a say.

(**Laurence** *goes.*)

Beverly Don't forget those light ales!

Laur. No—and the lagers.

Angela You going to take your test again?

Beverly Yeah, I'm going to have another try, yeah. Don't get me wrong, Tone, it's not that I can't drive—in fact I'm a good driver, but, let me put it to you this way, when I get to my test my nerves fail me, d'you know what I mean? I mean it was me nerves that failed me the last time, to be honest with you, because you know the way they take you out in threes. Tone, right? I started off behind this bloke—he was a Chinese bloke actually. Now, my bloke had told me to turn left, right? Now, we came to the first Give Way, and the bloke in front slammed his brakes on. Now, I'm going behind him, and I suppose I'm going a little bit too quick with me nerves; so I slam on my brakes, and I went slap in the back of him.

Angela Ah.

Beverly Now, I reckon that prejudiced my examiner against me.

Angela What a shame.

Beverly Yeah, it was, actually. Can you drive, Ang?

Angela No. I'd like to learn, but Tony won't let me. He doesn't think I'd be any good. And it's a shame, 'cos it's so awkward for me to get to work since we've moved.

Beverly Is it, yeah?

Angela And you see, I could use the car when he wasn't working.

Beverly And that would make you completely independent of Tone, wouldn't it?

(*Pause.*)

D'you pass your test first time, Tone?

Tony Yeah.

Beverly I thought so, actually—he looks the type, doesn't he? (*She goes to the bar.*) Who's for another drink? Ang?

Angela Thanks.

Beverly How about you, Tone?

Tony Ta.

Beverly Yeah? Great.

(*Laurence enters.*)

What's the matter?

Laur. Nothing. Tony, I wonder if you could give me a hand for a moment please?

Beverly Won't the car start?

Laur. No.

Angela Go on, Tony!

Tony All right!

(**Tony** *follows* **Laurence** *out*.)

Beverly Mind you don't go getting dirt on your suit. All right, Tone?

(**Beverly** *concludes pouring drinks*.)

Ang. (*passing the drink to her*)

Angela Thanks

Beverly Cheers.

Angela Cheers.

Beverly Ang—would you mind if I asked you a personal question?

Angela No.

Beverly Now, please don't be offended when I say this, but . . . can you take a little bit of criticism?

Angela (*after a brief pause*) Yes.

Beverly Now, okay. I can see what you've done: you've just sat down in front of your mirror, and you've put your lipstick on. Now, this is something I always used to tell my customers, and it always works. Now, next time, just sit down in front of your mirror, and relax. And just say to yourself, 'I've got very beautiful lips.' Then take your lipstick and apply it, and you'll see the difference, Ang. Because then you will applying your lipstick to every single corner of your mouth, d'you know what I mean? Will you try it for me next time?

Angela Yes.

Beverly Just sit down in front of your mirror, and relax, and say to yourself . . .

Angela 'I've got very beautiful lips.'

Beverly And I promise you you'll see the difference, Ang! Okay?

Angela Thanks.

(*The front door bell chimes.*)

Beverly Would you excuse me just one minute, Ang?

(**Beverly** *goes out*. **Angela** *helps herself to a cheese-pineapple savoury*.)

Beverly (*off*) Hi, Sue.

Susan (*off*) Hello, Beverly.

Beverly (*off*) Come in.

Susan (*off*) Thank you.

(*Beverly and Susan enter. Susan carries her handbag and a wrapped bottle.*)

Beverly All right, Sue?

Susan Yes, thank you.

Beverly Come through.

Susan I'm sorry I'm a bit late.

Beverly Now, don't worry, Sue, that's all right. Would you like to slip your jacket off?

Susan Oh, thank you.

Beverly Everything all right, Sue?

Susan Yes, I think so. I hope so.

Beverly Come through and say hullo. Ang, this is Sue. Sue, this is Ang.

Angela Hello.

Susan How d'you do.

Beverly Sue's from Number Nine.

Angela Oh, we've just moved into Number Sixteen.

Susan Oh, really?

Beverly Yeah, you know the Macdonalds' old house, Sue?

Susan Yes.

Beverly Yeah. Sit down Sue. I'll just pop your coat in the hall. (*going*) Won't be a sec. Make yourself at home, Sue!

(**Beverly** *exits with* **Susan***'s coat.*)

Susan Thank you. (*She puts the wrapped bottle on the bar, and proceeds to sit down putting her handbag on the floor.*)

Angela We've only been here a fortnight.

Susan Oh, really?

(**Beverly** *returns.*)

Beverly (*referring to the bottle*) Did you bring that, Sue?

Susan Yes.

Beverly Is it for us?

Susan Yes.

Beverly Oh, thank you, Sue!

Susan It's nothing very special, I'm afraid.

Beverly Ah. Isn't that kind, Ang?

Angela Yes.

Susan Not at all.

Beverly (*unwrappping the bottle*) Oh, lovely! 'Cos Laurence likes a drop of wine, actually. Oh, it's Beaujolais. Fantastic! Won't be a sec, I'll just pop it in the fridge. (*She goes to the kitchen.*)

Angela I'm so pleased to meet you. I want to meet all the neighbours.

Susan Yes.

(**Beverly** *returns.*)

Beverly Now Sue: what would you like to drink?
Susan I'll have a glass of sherry, please.
Beverly Sherry, are you sure?
Susan Yes. Thank you.
Beverly 'Cos we've got everything. There's gin, whisky, vodka, brand whatever you'd like. Would you like a little gin and tonic, Sue 'Cos me and Ang are drinking gin and tonic, actually.
Susan All right—thank you.
Beverly Ice and lemon?
Susan Yes please.
Beverly Great.

Points for discussion or written work

1. What examples can you find here of what might be called 'social competition', more commonly known as 'keeping-up-with-the-Joneses'?

2. How does Beverly dominate this scene ? Does she show any lack of taste, or insensitivity towards other people, and if so, how?

3. Can you discover any hints in this extract of any hidden tensions in the marriage of Beverly and Laurence?

4. Much emphasis is placed in this scene on 'social' drinking of alcohol. A definite pattern emerges—almost a ritual—in the giving and receiving of drinks. Study this carefully. Do you think that the author might have been making any social comment here? Does this happen in real life?

5. Why do you think Susan is given only short speeches, and Tony even less? How does Beverly show that she likes Tony?

6. What parts of this extract did you find amusing—and why?

Suggestions for script or improvisation

1. Improvise or script a scene where Sue tells one of her best friends about the awful evening with Beverly, Laurence, Angela and Tony. Try to include Sue's thoughts on each character. Do you think Sue might have liked any one character better than the others?

2. Set up a scene with Angela and Tony on their return home that evening. This could be an argument between them over what had happened.

Moving on from there . . .

3. Imagine some new neighbours have moved into the semi-detached house next door. You have invited them round for drinks, but as the evening progresses, it becomes very clear that you have little in common. (Think of some good reasons why this might be.) You

may include as many characters as you wish in this sketch.

4. Work together in a group of ten or so to create a lively party atmosphere, possibly with loud music and atmospheric lighting. You can decide your own age, but it should be no older than twenty-five. The party should be allowed to get going before a neighbour arrives to complain about noise (and also possibly things happening which are associated with the party: noisy car doors slamming etc.). He/she is from the house next door, and has lots of good reasons why the party should be ended. You decide what happens . . .

Stephen Poliakoff

City Sugar

The playwright Stephen Poliakoff, born in 1952, read history at Cambridge, but left at the end of his second year before taking his final exams. His first play, *Day With My Sister*, written while he was still at school, was first performed at the Traverse Theatre in Edinburgh in 1971. His first major success was *Clever Soldiers* in 1974, followed closely by *Hitting Town* and *City Sugar* in the same year. In 1976, he was appointed 'Writer in Residence' at The National Theatre, and in the same year won *The Evening Standard's* 'most promising' playwright award.

The play *City Sugar* asks us to consider the harmful effects of mindless pop radio, which, it suggests, can dull the thinking capacity of its audience. The central character, local disc-jockey Leonard Brazil, despises himself for delivering what he calls 'milk chocolate pap' in his programme each day, and the play tells of his desperate, and largely unsuccessful attempts to break out of the unsatisfactory lifestyle into which he has been forced. *The Times* called it 'a scathingly brilliant play'.

The extract Leonard Brazil's programme on Leicester Sound, a local commercial radio station.

Characters: how it might be acted

Leonard Brazil: *a smooth-talking DJ; self-important and quite aggressive; lacks sympathy for other people.*
Rex: *Leonard's sound engineer; very much in awe of Leonard.*
Angela/Rita/Nicola: *anonymous teenage voices; callers to Leonard's radio phone-in.*

Two areas should be created with tables—Leonard's broadcasting record desk console, and Rex's engineer's box.
Records mentioned could be updated.

(*The Studio.*
Leonard Brazil *is sitting at the record desk.* **Rex** *is in the engineer's box. Pop music plays as the house lights dim, and fades after the* **Curtain** *rises.*)

Leonard (*into the mike*) From nineteen sixty-eight, there, Amen Corner, featuring the unmistakable soprano of Mr André Fairweather-Low, and 'If Paradise Was Half As Nice'. Welcome back to the L.B. show. L.B.—the two most important initials in the country. L.B. on five hundred and fifty waves—that's a lot of water. (*Loudly*) *Five hundred and fifty* medium waves! (*He smiles.*) Sorry. 'You can do better than that, Brazil.' 'Yes, Boss.' In a few minutes we have something for you, something special. (*He begins to open the letters on the turntable desk.*) I want to say hello to those I met in North Street yesterday; people out in their gardens with *green* fingers, very definitely, and green feet, too, so I'm told. And one even with green hair. No, it was very nice meeting you. They have lovely gardens up there, don't they, lovely houses! (*In his more normal voice*) I have a few letters in front of me—I've been struggling to open. I have one from Mrs Lee, Mrs D. Lee, saying that did I know there was now a topless restaurant in this fine city of ours, and its name is the Aubergine—how's that for a free commercial, you guys over there in the Aubergine—and Mrs Lee wonders, what do I think about it? I think—it's a very classy name, *The Aubergine*, perhaps in French it is something more than just a vegetable. I wonder, since we're being blue—or blue*ish*, perhaps we could ask—would any of the ladies like to see bottomless waiters approaching you with your curry? Rex is suggesting a lot of rude vegetable jokes about what this restaurant would be called, which I will ignore. Enough of this smut. I went to the cinema yesterday, saw the very excellent 'Death Wish', a lot of rape and gore and blood and guts, for those of you that like your toast buttered that way—me, I prefer the lovely, the scintillating, the mind-expanding Lynsey De Paul. (*Over the beginning of the record, which he has switched on*) Nobody need fear—Lynsey De Paul is here . . . (*He turns the switch, after a few bars, the music is now playing silently while the record goes round. He drops the biro on the desk. A pause.*) That was execrable. (*He flicks the intercom to speak to* **Rex** *in the box.*) That was a real stinker. A loosener—

and a very loose loosener at that. (*Pause; he continues into the intercom*) Come in here . . . It's the sleepy time for them at the moment, all gorged after Sunday lunch, lying in heaps round the room—they won't want to be stirred. (*Pause: louder, into the intercom*) Get yourself in here, right now!

(**Rex** *enters behind him.*)

Rex I'm here.

Leonard That's better.

Rex I've brought a drink.

Leonard How kind . . . (*with a slight smile*) Trying to placate me, are you? What is it?

Rex Lime juice; it's a free sample of one of the commercials we're carrying this week. I thought you'd like to try it.

Leonard It looks like a congealed shampoo. (*He puts it to one side. Suddenly staring at* **Rex**; *loudly*) Now, why haven't you filled these up?

Rex I was going to.

Leonard Going to! Everybody keeps on telling me how efficient you are, how fortunate I am to have you. I have yet to notice. Go and do these now. (*He hands him sheets of record titles to be filled in.*) I warn you, it's a particularly grisly lot. (*Smiling*) I seem to have played pap for an entire week—might as well have stuck the stylus into cotton-wool.

(**Rex** *moves slightly.*)

And why hasn't my mail been checked . . . ?

Rex (*embarrassed*) Sorry, I . . .

Leonard (*holding up a letter*) I've been asked to open another municipal pleasure pond—which is completely out of the question, of course.

Rex. Why?

Leonard (*riffling through his other letters*) The last time—the one and only time I had to baptize a pond—it was in front of councillors and crowds, and all the rest—and I had to launch it—with a champagne bottle, containing—(*suddenly looking up*)—and this is completely and utterly true—frog spawn. A bottleful. I wasn't allowed to smash it against the side, of course, I had to solemnly pour it out, and of course the bloody stuff got stuck and I had to stand there shaking it, and banging the bottom, like a ketchup bottle, until, of course, I got it all over myself. (*He looks up.*) What I really hate is somebody that doesn't believe a good true story. (*Loudly*) Get on with it!

(**Rex** *moves slightly.*)

(*Loudly*) What's more, I've never seen a single person even *near* that pond—thousands of pounds spent on a small, windswept hole in completely the wrong place.

Rex I—By the way—I've left an item there—(*indicating the desk*)—you might like.

Leonard You have, have you? Worse and worse, Rex. You're having a good day, aren't you? (*Smiling*) I don't like suggestions very much, you should know that by now.

Rex Yeah, but I thought—you could—I wanted . . .

Leonard No!

(**Rex** *exits.*)

(*He turns suddenly to the mike, turns on a record over the monitor speakers and fades it down.*) That was Miss De Paul. I'm now struggling with another letter on pink paper—it's from Mrs Joan Parsons saying 'Dear Leonard, is it true or false that you were a teacher in another life?' Well, now, I don't know about another life, Joan, but I was in this one, yes. I trained as a teacher as it happens, before I slipped into the record business, and when all that went up in a puff of smoke, I slipped back into the classroom, until of course I heard the call of Leicester Sound. I thought that everybody knew that, Joan. (*Smiling*) A joke. And a note here from a theatre group calling itself the Gracious Players, saying, could I give a free plug to their production of Dame Agatha Christie's *Towards Zero* on Saturday at the Town Hall, Hinkley, which seats one thousand five hundred people. No wonder they wanted their free mention. And I'm now being handed by the ever-dependable Rex, a piece of paper on which is written 'DON'T FORGET'. And if you don't know what that means, I do, and I'll tell you in a moment, for we have a real thriller coming up; but to change the subject—(*putting on a record*)—I have lost some weight. In fact I've lost so much weight, I'm floating out of my seat, floating round the studio. (*Ghost-story medium voice*) They've had to weigh down my trousers with *Encyclopaedia Britannicas.* (*In his normal voice*) While our friend Rex is gaining all the time, I'm afraid, he's approaching sixteen stone now, a hunky piece of flesh, can hardly fit into his box. Enough of this gibberish. DON'T FORGET means competition time. We have a stunner for you in a moment—till then, let's flash back into the dim distant past of last week. (*He switches on a record, 'It's Gonna Sell A Million'; he turns it off after a couple of bars.*) That was better—that was very slightly better. (*He gets up and walks.*)

(*Rex enters.*)

Rex Why do you keep on doing this?

Leonard Doing what?

Rex You know . . .

Leonard Putting weight on you, you mean—making you an obese lump. It's my rather dismal little joke.

Rex I thought—you were the one for truth over the air.

Leonard I allow myself this one slight distortion.

Rex But people will discover, won't they?

Leonard No they won't, nobody's ever going to publish a picture of you, are they?

Rex Yes. (*Pause*) The local press might.

Leonard (*smiling*) Not with shares in this station they won't. In fact a total wall of silence could be preserved about your real size for evermore. In fact if I wanted I could pump you up steadily to twenty-five stone, and then burst you. (*Pause*) Sorry. (*Smiling*) Don't worry, I do it to everyone that works for me.

Rex So I've heard.

Leonard So there's no need to look injured. You're not, yet.

(**Rex** *moves to go.*)

Rex (*with a slight smile*) By the way, I've got Capitol on the line.

Leonard (*without looking up*) You'll have to be more convincing than that. Been listening to jabber and gossip, have you?

Rex I suppose so, yes.

Leonard Well don't.

Rex (*watching him*) Everybody knows, anyway. Are they going to make an offer, then?

Leonard It's just possible. Everything's possible. I shouldn't bank on it.

Rex For the afternoon show . . . (*smiling*) They'll be sending spies up here. They'll be sitting in pubs with transistors and earplugs, listening away. You'll have to give them the whole works.

Leonard (*not looking up*) Will I . . . Get it ready.

Rex It is ready.

Leonard (*totally matter-of-fact*) You can have a moment longer than usual, because I'm in a generous mood.

Rex Thanks—I——

Leonard (*cutting him off, swinging round to the mike and switching on the monitor speakers; fading down the end of the record*) And now, a special competition. You heard me—a mind-tingling competition. And by my side is the ever-dependable Rex, sweating slightly, what have we got as a prize, Rex?

Rex (*nervously, standing by the mike and speaking into it; putting on* *almost a BBC voice*) We have *their* latest LP—the Yellow Jacks' latest!

Leonard (*in a brash voice*) Tell us the title, Rex—*please* tell us the title.

Rex 'Somewhere Up There.'

Leonard That's a fine title—is it a fine record?

Rex It's very exciting, Leonard, it really is . . .

Leonard (*to the listeners*) And you can have it a whole two or three weeks before it's in the shops, one of the very first in the whole country to have it. And what is Rex going to make us do? Well, I think he's been fiddling with his tapes.

Rex I have indeed . . .

Leonard Very posh today, aren't we, Rex?

Rex Are we, Leonard?

Leonard And what have you done with your tapes?

Rex I've slowed them down—rather a lot.

Leonard Slowed them down—we're getting even more posh.

Rex Yes.

Leonard (*loudly*) Tell me, Rex, what affect does this have on the listener?

Rex What?

Leonard (*very fast*) What effect does this have on the *listener*?

Rex What—well it . . . (*He dries completely and stands helpless*) I . . (**Leonard** *presses a button: a tape of Leicester Sound jingle cuts off* **Rex**'*s floundering.* **Rex** *returns to his box.*)

Leonard Enough of this gibberish. (*In his normal voice*) O.K., sweets—this is it. Rex is going to play one of the songs in the Top *Eleven*, and it has been sl-o-o-o-owed do-o-o-own, so it sounds a little different. And you're going to give us the singer and the song, aren't you. Double-five-three-zero-four—is the number to ring—that's right. (*In a Bogart voice*) Play it again, Rex. (**Rex**, *back in his box, switches on a tape of 'The Pround One' by the Osmonds, at 16 r.p.m.;after a few bars, reducing the volume on the monitor speakers; talking into the intercom to* **Rex**; *off the air*) Sounds a little more exciting like this, doesn't it. I shall always play it like this in future. (*Suddenly, loudly*) All records will be played at *eight* R.P.M., and we'll talk that slowly, too. (**Rex** *comes out of the box.*)

Rex I'm—I'm sorry about messing things up, I didn't mean to . . .

Leonard Of course you didn't . . .

Rex You took me by surprise, I didn't think . . . I'm sorry, I won't do it again.

Leonard No, of course you won't. You won't get another chance to. Now get back into your box where you belong.

(**Rex** *returns to the box.* **Leonard** *switches the mike to go live again, and speaks loudly.*)

Rex—what have you done to my favourite song? How's that for first-degree murder—a fine song slo-o-o-owly tortured to death. O.K., sweets, who can be the first caller—race to your phones, dial furiously. I'm touching the first prize now—all fourteen tracks of it—we're handling the two of them with rubber gloves up here—and forceps, and we're keeping them in an incubator at night, in case we can hatch a third. Seriously now—(*he puts headphones on*)—we have a caller; and the first caller is . . .

A Girl (*on the telephone, amplified through monitors*) Hello . . .

Leonard (*softly*) Hello there—what's your name, love?

Girl Angela

Leonard Lovely. Have we ever talked before?

Angela No, never.

Leonard Fine. You at home, Angela?

Angela Yeah—I'm at home.

Leonard Good—well, let's go straight into it, Angela, into the unknown . . .

(*He signals to* **Rex**, *who switches on the slowed-down tape again, in the background.*)

Who do you think the noise is, this *slo-o-ow* noise?

Angela Is it—'The Proud One' by the Osmonds?

Leonard Did you say . . .

Angela (*about to correct herself*) I——

Leonard (*interrupting*) Angela, you're r-r-r-o-o-o-ight! Well done!

(**Rex** *speeds up the record to the right speed; it plays a few bars;* **Leonard** *signals to* **Rex** *and the volume is reduced.*)

There we go—clever girl. I'm dropping your prize into Rex's hand, to be wiped spotless, and posted, jet-propelled, towards you, Angela. 'Bye, love. Let's have the next one, Rex.

(*A slowed-down version of 'Na Na Is the Saddest Word' by the Stylistics.* **Leonard** *gets up again.* **Rex** *comes out of the box.*)

This is an easy kill for them—they use their record-players so much at home, they all run slow anyway—those who *have* record-players.

Rex (*staring at* **Leonard**) I really like it, you know—(*with a slight smile*)—*if* I'm allowed to say so, how you always touch something when you're talking about it, even if it's the wrong record, like just now. (*He returns to the box.*)

Leonard Yes. I like that, too. It's the actor in me. It's what makes it reasonably good. (*Staring round the studio*) Where is the nauseating object, anyway? (*He sees the Yellow Jacks' L.P. and picks up up*) Have you read the back, with Ross—(*in an American film-trailer voice*)—the leader singer speaking *his mind*—(*in his normal voice*)—take an example at random—and this is a nice lad from Bolton speaking—'Ross numbers among his favourite things; walnut ice-cream, honeysuckle, genuine people, starfish, and sunburnt bare feet.' (*Loudly*) You realize we're going to have to play the utterances of this jellied imbecile all this week—the promoters have sent us a long tape, in a silk case, and the station's excited, too, they want it to be a lively few days, I keep getting little illiterate messages pushed under the door saying 'Please remember, *maximum* required'. (*Switching on the mike suddenly*) Hello—what's your name, please?

A Girl Rita.

Leonard (*with a slight smile*) Lovely Rita Meter Maid.

Rita What?

Leonard A reference to years gone by, don't let it worry you, Rita. Have we talked before?

Rita No.

Leonard You listen often . . .

Rita Yes—yes I do.

Leonard (*smiling, softly*) Good, that's how it should be. Let's go straight into it then, love, into the nitty-gritty—who do you think it is?

Rita I think it's 'Whole Lot of Loving' by Guys and Dolls. (*She gives the wrong title.*)

Leonard Well, Rita, you're wrong, I'm afraid.

Rita No I'm not—am I?

Leonard I'm afraid so.

Rita You sure? (*Louder*) I was certain. You——

Leonard (*cutting her off*) I'm sorry, love, you're wrong; keep listening though, for a very important reason—'bye for now. (*In a Hughie Green voice*) And let's go straight on to the next contestant! Coming up to Big John with the news at three o'clock. One down, one L.P. to go—round, crisp and shiny. What's your name, please?

Nicola Hello.

Leonard A little louder please—what's your name?

Nicola (*very quietly*) Nicola Davies.

Leonard A little louder.

Nicola (*loudly*) Nicola Davies.

Leonard Nicola Davies. That's very formal. Are you at home, Nicola Davies?

Nicola Yes.

Leonard And what are you wearing, Nicola?

Nicola I—trousers . . .

Leonard A little louder—you've got a very nice voice, Nicola. You're wearing trousers; and anything else?

Nicola Yes—shoes.

Leonard Shoes, that's an interesting picture, she's wearing just trousers and shoes. Only wish we had television phones, sexy Nicola—so, to win this L.P., that Rex is just slipping into its beautiful see-through, tight-fitting sleeve—who is it, Nicola?

Nicola It's the Stylistics and 'Na Na is the Saddest Sound'. (*She gives the wrong title.*)

Leonard I'm afraid, Nicola——

Nicola (*interrupting, correcting herself*) No, it's 'The Saddest Word'.

Leonard Well, Nicola—I'm afraid, your first answer is the only one I can accept . . .

Nicola Oh . . .

Leonard But you were very close—and so, as you've given us *all* your name, Nicola Davis—I'm going, actually, to give it to you.

Nicola Oh good—thank you.

Leonard Just for you, Nicola Davis, but on one condition—and that is . . .

Nicola (*nervously*) What is that?

Leonard You listen for just one more moment, because I have something rather extraordinary to announce to you and to everyone. I'm going to be running many competitions this week for all ages—but one of them is different—for, to tie in with the great Yellow Jacks' concert here in this city on Satuday—we're running THE COMPETITION OF THE CENTURY—and the prize is actually meeting one of the boys. How do you like that, Nicola Davies?

Nicola Yes—what do you do?

Leonard And not only that—the winner will ride to London, after the concert, in *their* car, sitting with *them*, and what is more they will then spend four whole days in London, the capital of this fine country, at the expense of Leicester Sound. That's O.K., isn't it, Nicola?

Nicola Yes—what do——

Leonard (*cutting her off*) So everybody tune in tomorrow, for the first stage—you too, Nicola—(*smiling*) you never know—what your luck might be. We might even speak again. (*He puts down the phone and drops his biro on the desk.*)

The Lights fade to a **Black-out**.

Points for discussion or written work

1. What differences can you discover between Leonard when he is 'on the air' and when he is not?

2. How does Leonard treat Rex, his engineer? Why does he lie about Rex's appearance? What is Rex's attitude to Leonard?

3. What does Leonard feel about the products advertised on Leicester Sound and the material he has to include in his shows?

4. How would you describe Leonard's conversation with Nicola, the final contestant? Does he give her a fair chance? What impression do we get of Leonard's attitude to his audience from this exchange, and from anything else he says here?

5. Does this radio programme sound like any you might have heard? Can you think of any similar examples?

6. Rex uses the term 'truth over the air'. When and why might it be dangerous to believe without question all we hear on radio or see and hear on television?

7. Imagine you are the Programme Controller of a small local radio station, serving your own area. Make up a good name for the station, and write out a plan for a complete week's programmes. Include full timing and names of programmes together with fictitious names of presenters and performers taking part. Beside each programme write a couple of sentences saying what it might include.

8. Write a correctly set out letter to the same Programme Controller of your radio station complaining about some feature of the station which you dislike. Make sure that the letter is really convincing! Remember to include both your name and address and that of the Radio Station and its Programme Controller.

Suggestions for script or improvisation

1. Set up a scene with Leonard and Rex working on a programme called 'Problem Phone-In' where callers speak to Leonard about a problem that is troubling them. How would Leonard react to them both on and off the air? Try to show the difference between the public and the private Leonard.

2. Improvise the scene where Leonard is called to the Programme Controller's office to answer several complaints that he has received about Leonard and his programme.

3. Improvise, or script Leonard making a public appearance, possibly opening a new supermarket or record shop. Use as many 'extras' as you can find to make this scene as lively and realistic as possible.

Moving on from there . . .

4. Write or improvise your own radio programme sequence and include a section where listeners telephone in to talk to the presenter, either in response to a radio quiz or for opinions on a current news item. You might then want to record it.

5. Devise, and if possible record, some radio advertisements that could be featured in the above programme. Use some of these as the names of suitable products:
COBUNUT : NUIT D'AMOUR : FLANGE! : CREATION

The Right to Live - or to Die

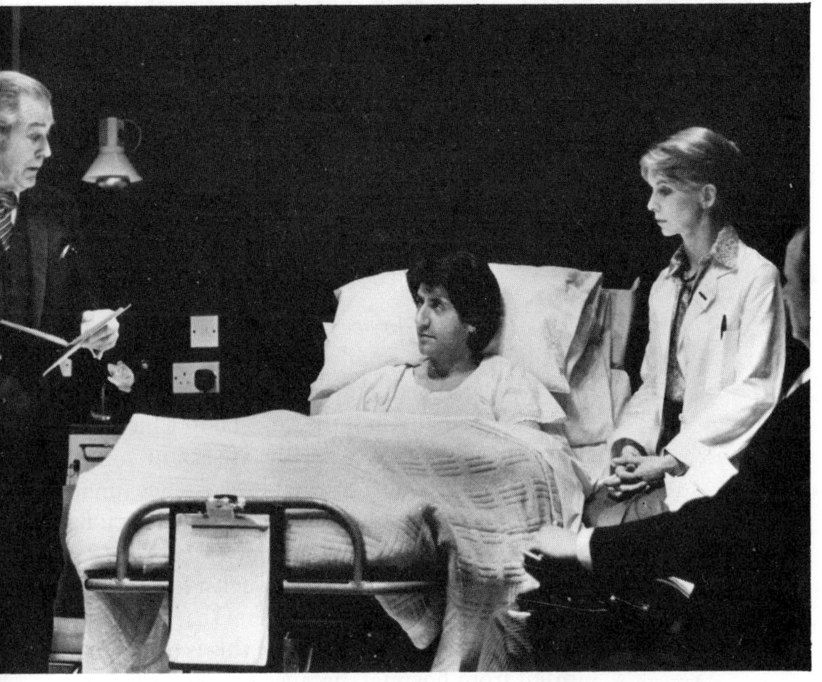

The final extract, from the play *Whose Life is it Anyway?* stands on its own because, although few people will ever in their lives experience the devastating injury suffered by its main character, everyone should consider the deeper issue: the question of personal freedom that is the play's central theme.

How free are we, as individuals, to decide for ourselves the course our lives will follow? What things outside ourselves shape our destiny? What do we mean by 'personal freedom' anyway?

Brian Clark

Whose Life is it Anyway?

The playwright Brian Clark, born in 1932, a trained teacher and actor, has written over twenty plays for television, including: *Achilles Heel, Operation, The Country Party, There's No Place*, and *Happy Returns*. This play, *Whose Life Is It Anyway?*, revised and rewritten in 1978, was presented on the West End stage in that year, with the actor Tom Conti as the central character. It was a critical and commercial success, and was subsequently taken on tour in the provinces and to America.

The play *Whose Life Is It Anyway?* is the story of Ken Harrison, a sculptor, who is totally paralysed as a result of a car crash. He is so badly injured that only his brain can function normally, but the hospital to which he is taken after the accident saves his life. He is now condemned in his own words to a 'vegetable' existence, unable to control his broken body, but fully and consciously aware of what he feels is the hopelessness of his situation. Ken cannot face such a future and makes very carefully considered decision that he wishes to die.

The only way he can achieve this is by discharging himself from hospital, because he could not exist without medical treatment. However, as he is completely helpless physically, he must gain the consent of the hospital authorities to be allowed to leave. In the end, he has to summon legal help to achieve this and the climax of the play consists of a special court held in the hospital when a judge has to decide whether Ken will be condemned to life in hospital—or be allowed to leave, and die.

The play was described as 'a great rarity in our theatre' by Irving Wardle, drama critic of *The Times*, because its subject matter—a discussion of the pros and cons of euthanasia, the medical termination of life—is a 'non-political social issue' and such themes have recently been much more the concern of television rather than the theatre. Wardle gave *Whose Life is it Anyway?* his 'strongest' recommendation, adding that it was 'quite a thrill to be back in a theatre buzzing with interest over a question of real public importance'.

The extract Ken's room in the hospital. He has learnt that he will always depend on other people for every physical function, and lies helpless in bed. The night before he had been forcibly injected with valium, a tranquillizer. This is the only treatment—to give Ken large doses of mind-numbing drugs—that the hospital can suggest to alleviate his desperate situation.

Characters: how it might be acted

Ken: *although he is physically paralysed, Ken's mind is extremely lively and intelligent; he has a sharp, witty tongue; he is fairly young, mid-thirties.*
Sister Anderson: *cool and professional on the surface, but caring also.*
Nurse Kay Sadler: *more openly warm than Sister, she had become quite attached to Ken, and involved in his situation.*
Mrs Gillian Boyle: *medical social worker, 35, very detached and professional in her manner.*

Use chairs joined together or blocks to suggest Ken's hospital bed.

Whose Life is it Anyway?

(*Ken Harrison's hospital bedroom.* **Ken** *is alone, in bed.* **Sister** *and* **Kay** *come in with the trolley.*)

Sister Good morning, Mr Harrison. How are you this morning?
Ken Marvellous.
Sister Night Sister said you slept well.
Ken I did. I had a lot of help, remember.
Sister Your eyes are bright this morning.
Ken I've been thinking.
Sister You do too much of that.
Ken What other activity would you suggest? Football? I tell you

what, Sister, just leave me alone with Nurse Sadler here. Let's see what the old Adam can do for me.

Sister I'm a sister, not a madam.

Ken Sister—you dark horse you! All this time you've been kidding me. I've been wondering for months how on earth a woman could become a State Registered Nurse and a Sister and still think you found babies under a gooseberry bush—and you've known all along.

Sister Of course I've known. When I qualified as a midwife I learnt that when they pick up the babies from under the gooseberry bushes they wrap them up in women to keep them warm. I know because it was our job to unwrap them again.

Ken The miracle of modern science! Anyway, Sister, as I said, I've been thinking, if I'm going to be around for a long time, money will help.

Sister It always does.

Ken Do you remember that solicitor chap representing my insurance company a few months ago? Mr Hill, I think he said his name was. He said he'd come back when I felt better. Do you think you could get him back as soon as possible? I'd feel more settled if we could get the compensation sorted out.

Sister Sounds a good idea.

Ken You'll ring him up?

Sister Of course.

Ken He left a card; it's in my drawer.

Sister Right. (*She goes to the locker and takes out a card.*) 'Mr Philip Hill, Solicitor.' Right, I'll ring him.

Ken Thanks.

Sister That's enough.
(*They straighten the bed.*)
Mrs Boyle is waiting to see you, Mr Harrison.

Ken Mrs Boyle? Who's she?

Sister A very nice woman.

Ken Oh God, must I see her?

Sister Dr Emerson asked her to come along.

Ken Then I'd better see her, if I refuse he'll probably dissolve her in water and inject her into me.
(**Sister** *has to choke back a giggle.*)

Sister Mr Harrison! Come on, Nurse, this man will be the death of me.

Ken (*cheerfully*) Doubt it, Sister; I'm not even able to be the death of myself.

(**Sister** *goes out with* **Kay**. **Gillian Boyle** *enters. She is thirty-five, attractive and very professional in her manner. She is a medical social worker.*)

Mrs B. Good morning.

Ken 'Morning.

Mrs B. Mr Harrison?

(**Sister** *enters her office.*)

Ken (*cheerfully*) It used to be.

Mrs B. My name is Mrs Boyle.

Ken And you've come to cheer me up.

Mrs B. I wouldn't put it like that.

Ken How would you put it?

Mrs B. I've come to see if I can help.

Ken Good. You can.

Mrs B. How?

Ken Go and convince Dr Frankenstein that he has successfully made his monster and he can now let it go.

Mrs B. Dr Emerson is a first-rate physician. My goodness, they have improved this room.

Ken Have they?

Mrs B. It used to be really dismal. All dark green and cream. It's surprising what pastel colours will do isn't it? Really cheerful.

Ken Yes; perhaps they should try painting me. I'd hate to be the thing that ruins the décor.

Mrs B. What on earth makes you say that? You don't ruin anything.

Ken I'm sorry. That was a bit—whining. Well, don't let me stop you.

Mrs B. Doing what?

Ken What you came for I suppose. What do you do? Conjuring tricks? Funny stories? Or a belly dance? If I had any choice, I'd prefer the belly dance.

Mrs B. I'm afraid I've left my bikini at home.

Ken Who said anything about a bikini.

Mrs B. Dr Emerson tells me that you don't want any more treatment.

Ken Good.

Mrs B. Why good?

Ken I didn't think he'd heard what I'd said.

Mrs B. Why not?

Ken He didn't take any notice.

Mrs B. Well, as you can see, he did.

Ken He sent you?

Mrs B. Yes.

Ken And you are my new treatment; get in.
Mrs B. Why don't you want any more treatment?
Ken I'd rather not go on living like this.
Mrs B. Why not?
Ken Isn't it obvious?
Mrs B. Not to me. I've seen many patients like you.
Ken And they all want to live?
Mrs B. Usually.
Ken Why?
Mrs B. They find a new way of life.
Ken How?
Mrs B. You'll be surprised how many things you will be able to do with training and a little patience.
Ken Such as?
Mrs B. We can't be sure yet. But I should think that you will be able to operate reading machines and perhaps an adapted typewriter.
Ken Reading and writing. What about arithmetic?
Mrs B. (*smiling*) I dare say we could fit you up with a comptometer if you really wanted one.
Ken Mrs Boyle, even educationalists have realized that the three r's do not make a full life.
Mrs B. What did you do before the accident?
Ken I taught in an Art School. I was a sculptor.
Mrs B. I see.
Ken Difficult, isn't it? How about an electrically operated hammer and chisel? No, well. Or a cybernetic lump of clay?
Mrs B. I wouldn't laugh if I were you. It's amazing what can be done. Our scientists are wonderful.
Ken They are. But it's not good enough you see, Mrs Boyle. I really have absolutely no desire at all to be the object of scientific virtuosity. I have thought things over very carefully. I do have plenty of time for thinking and I have decided that I do not want to go on living with so much effort for so little result.
Mrs B. Yes, well, we shall have to see about that.
Ken What is there to see?
Mrs B. We can't just stop treatment, just like that.
Ken Why not?
Mrs B. It's the job of the hospital to save life, not to lose it.
Ken The hospital's done all it can, but it wasn't enough. It wasn't the hospital's fault; the original injury was too big.
Mrs B. We have to make the best of the situation.
Ken No. 'We' don't have to do anything. I have to do what is to be

done, and that is to cash in the chips.

Mrs B. It's not unusual you know for people injured as you have been to suffer with this depression for a considerable time before they begin to see that a life is possible.

Ken How long?

Mrs B. It varies.

Ken Don't hedge.

Mrs B. It could be a year or so.

Ken And it could last for the rest of my life.

Mrs B. That would be most unlikely.

Ken I'm sorry, but I cannot settle for that.

Mrs B. Try not to dwell on it. I'll see what I can do to get you started on some occupational therapy. Perhaps we could make a start on the reading machines.

Ken Do you have many books for those machines?

Mrs B. Quite a few.

Ken Can I make a request for the first one.

Mrs B. If you like.

Ken 'How to be a sculptor with no hands.'

Mrs B. I'll be back tomorrow with the machine.

Ken It's marvellous, you know.

Mrs B. What is?

Ken All you people have the same technique. When I say something really awkward you just pretend I haven't said anything at all. You're all the bloody same . . . Well, there's another outburst. That should be your cue to comment on the lightshade or the colour of the walls.

Mrs B. I'm sorry if I have upset you.

Ken Of course you have upset me. You and the doctors with your appalling so-called professionalism, which is nothing more than a series of verbal tricks to prevent you relating to your patients as human beings.

Mrs B. You must understand; we have to remain relatively detached in order to help . . .

Ken That's all right with me. Detach yourself. Tear yourself off on the dotted line that divides the woman from the social worker and post yourself off to another patient.

Mrs B. You're very upset . . .

Ken Christ Almighty, you're doing it again. Listen to yourself, woman. I say something offensive about you and you turn your professional cheek. If you were human, if you were treating me as human, you'd tell me to bugger off. Can't you see that this is why I've decided that life isn't worth living. I am not human, and I'm even more convinced of that by your visit than I was before, so how does that grab you? The very exercise of your so-called professionalism makes me want to die.

Mrs B. I'm—please . . .

Ken Go—for God's sake get out—go on—get out—get out.

(**Mrs Boyle** *goes into* **Sister***'s room.* **Sister** *hears* **Ken***'s shouts.*)

Sister What's the matter, Mrs Boyle?

Mrs B. It's Mr Harrison—he seems very upset.

Ken (*shouting*) I am upset.

(**Sister** *closes the door.*)

Sister I should leave him for now, Mrs Boyle. We'll send for you again when he's better.

(**Mrs Boyle** *hovers in the corridor.* **Sister** *hurries in to* **Ken**, **Ken** *is very distressed, rocking his head from side to side, desperately short of breath.*)

Ken Sis—ter . . .

(**Sister** *reaches for the oxygen mask.*)

Sister Now, now, Mr Harrison, calm down.

(*She applies the mask and turns on the oxygen.* **Ken** *gradually becomes calmer.*)

Now why do you go getting yourself so upset—there's no point.

(**Kay** *enters the corridor.*)

Ken (*muffled*) But . . .

Sister Stop talking, Mr Harrison, just relax.

(**Ken** *becomes calm.* **Sister** *sees* **Kay** *going past.* **Mrs Boyle** *is still hovering.*)

Nurse.

Kay Sister? (*She enters* **Ken***'s room*)

Sister Take over here will you?

Kay Yes, Sister.

(**Kay** *holds the mask.* **Sister** *goes to the door.*)

Mrs B. Is he all right?

Sister Yes, perfectly.

Mrs B. I'm sorry . . .

Sister Don't worry, it was not you—we'll let you know when he's better.

Mrs B. Right—thank you.

(**Mrs Boyle** *goes.* **Sister** *stands at the open door.*)

Sister Just give him another ten seconds, Nurse.

Kay Yes, Sister.

(**Sister** *takes a pace back behind the door and listens. After ten* *seconds,* **Kay** *removes the mask.*)

Ken Oh, she's a shrewd cookie, is our Sister.
(**Sister** *smiles at this.* **Kay** *glances backward.* **Ken** *catches on to the reason.*)
It's all right, Sister, I'm still alive, bugger it. I don't want to give her too much satisfaction.
(**Sister** *goes.*)

Kay She's gone. (*She closes the door.*)

Ken Come on then, over here. I shan't bite you, Kay. Come and cool my fevered brow or something.

Kay What upset you?

Ken Being patronized I suppose.

Kay What did you mean about Sister?

Ken She knew if she came in I'd shout at her, but if you were here I wouldn't shout.

Kay Why?

Ken A good question. Because I suppose you're young and gentle and innocent, and Sister knows that I am not the sort who would shout at you . . .

Kay You mean, you would rather patronize me.

Ken Hey! Steady on there, Kay. If you show you're well able to take care of yourself I shall have to call you Nurse Sadler and shout at you too, and Sister and I will have lost a valuable asset.

Points for discussion or written work

1. Do you find Ken's humour in this situation hard to accept? Would an audience have been embarrassed by his ability to joke despite being injured—or does the playwright create more sympathy for Ken by making him joke about his situation?

2. Describe Ken's relationship with his two nurses. How did Sister Anderson differ from Nurse Sadler?

3. Can you draw any conclusions about Ken's character. How it might have been altered by his accident.

4. Mrs Boyle is described as being 'very professional in her manner'. How is this revealed here? Did she deal with Ken unsatisfactorily? Do you think she made any mistakes in her conversation with Ken? Can you

suggest anything she might have said, or done, which would have helped Ken more?

5. At the end of this extract, Ken says he felt he was being 'patronized'. What did he mean by this? Was he, and if so, how?

6. Had Ken, in wanting to end his life, made the correct decision?

7. *Life* and *Exit* are two organizations that represent contrasting opinions on the question of voluntary euthanasia. Find out as much as you can about the arguments that each put forward, and try to suggest what each would say about Ken's case. Organize a debate around this important subject.

Suggestions for script or improvisation

1. Improvise or script a scene between Ken and the girl friend he had before his accident, Meg. She is visiting him for only the second time. When she had last seen him he had been too ill to speak much; now he has had time to recover and is able to tell her and discuss with her his plans for the future . . . .

Moving on from there . . .

2. A hospital social worker interviews an old man or woman to decide if he/she can return home after a spell in hospital. The interview could reveal how lonely the old person was; it might portray the security offered by hospital life; it could show how hard-pressed and busy many of our hospitals are today.

3. Improvise or script a scene which shows how sometimes nurses or doctors forget that they are dealing with human beings.

4. Use the titles 'A Difficult Decision' or 'Hoping for Good News' as starters for script or improvisation.